War & Memories

Survival
With a
Measure of Success

By

Gary Clemmons

WHO IS GARY CLEMMONS

Anxious to live life to its fullest upon serving four years in the Marines, Gary rushed into things he felt passionate about. After surviving as a combat marine in Vietnam, he caddied on the West Coast Swing's PGA tour for a few years. He embarked on a Radio career that included disc-jockey work and jingle production and, although Gary had successful careers in both radio and construction, he was always involved in music. He has produced hit records, had songs placed in movies and TV and was band leader for Country Music Hall of Fame artist Johnny Western.

Gary obtained his General Contractor's license in 2000 and has built over 2 dozen multi-family housing projects. Today, although officially retired, because of his reputation as a highly skilled Contractor, he is often asked to be a consultant on major construction projects.

Clemmons has few regrets as he looks back on his life. In this autobiography, he has revisited the good times and the bad, the successes and the struggles. He has shared, as best he can, those moments of clarity that have helped him make sense of the path his life has taken after a combat tour. Most importantly he has allowed himself to gain some peace and understanding.

Gary's hope is that by sharing his story, it will inspire at least a few of America's current returning combat veterans to never lose hope.

In a combat zone one will learn to embrace each day as if it could be your last. The urgency and the rush, along with a noticeably more serious outlook experienced in combat, becomes natural behavior when each day presents a challenge to survive. This acute awareness did not come with an off and on switch. It lingers with intensity and becomes a major part of a personality. There is an invisible shield emblazoned with the caveat, "They are out to get me" across the top and "Be prepared to act first" across the bottom. Most veterans who have experienced a war zone will remain in a state of paranoia unless they seek counseling.

PTSD, you say? What is it and what are the symptoms? It can vary for each individual. But studies have also discovered there are several similarities.

Many returning combat veterans have had broken homes and multiple marriages. They have worked in several different professions and suffer from serious episodes of depression. Some have a very difficult time making good decisions and achieving goals so become prone to serious personality disorders.

Gary's hope is that by sharing his story, it will inspire a few of America's current returning combat veterans to never lose hope.

The memories, stories, and recollections in this memoir are unique to the author. His personal decisions along with planned and unplanned experiences have shaped a unique individual just as your actions have defined who you are today. But in many ways we are all the same.

We want to be happy and respected with whom we are. Some will deny it, but we all want to feel accepted and loved. Many veterans learn to only allow a certain level of closeness.

As we interact with each other through life's journey, let's have some compassion for others and occasionally whisper, "It could have been me".

It is a privilege to have been able to serve our country so now that we have, let's get busy living!

ONE OF THE FIVE

You can count on one hand

Endorsements and testimonials from various doctors, counselors, professional career acquaintances and others are readily available. But, one from someone who has been with you through the good and rocky times serves up an extreme amount of credibility. Following is a statement from one of Gary's closest friends Michael Fennello. Together they experienced life in real time. Forty-five years of understanding each other mostly with silent appreciation on both sides.

On the outside we looked so different, and our personal experiences to date had been polar opposites. As friends go we are definitely the best of. I met Gary Clemmons at Phoenix, Arizona Sky Harbor International Airport in 1971. Our wives (at the time) were best friends, so they sent Gary to pick me up at the airport. I'd later learn this would be the first time he'd returned to the airport since being deposited there 48-hours after intense struggles to stay alive in Vietnam at the front. We walked towards each other easily recognizing one another by our wives' descriptions. I with hair half-way down my back, and him still sporting a military buzz cut. On the way home that evening Gary took me to a cowboy bar; seemed like he was testing me, plopping this hippie into a red-neck world. To Gary's surprise, I knew a lot of people there too. I could feel him watching me as I said hi too many friends. I looked at him, totally at ease, and he looked back, shocked. I grinned, and then he did too. We've shared an inside joke ever since.

Some have said odd friendship, yet we had many things in common. We both loved golf, and began decades of playing and organizing tournaments together. Being the serious soldier, Gary didn't smoke marijuana. The first time I convinced him to try it, a smile came over his face like I'd never seen. He laughed and must have instantly felt relief. It was a new day.

After a time, our soon-to-be ex-wives said, "You guys spend so much time with each other, why not just move in together so you can play golf and get stoned whenever you want." That sounded like a great idea, so we did. We helped each other survive divorce, well on our way to a life-long friendship.

Gary liked hanging-out with my boisterous sisters and others in my three-generation Italian household. He mentioned feeling accepted there. No one treated him differently or tip-toed around the war, like a lot of people during that time. I think we helped him relax and chill out, just connect with living again in a safe space.

The Marines taught Gary a lot of skills, but 'how to relax' was not one of them. They taught him to be leery of anyone, and that if he didn't watch his back and those of his men, they could die. During the early years he pushed people away, partied a lot, and often worked day and night. So one day, tired of seeing Gary so uptight, I said, "Clem, let's go caddying on the PGA tour." He said, "What???" He thought I was nuts. After a time I convinced him to come with me to Phoenix Country Club and sign-up to caddy part-time for tour golfers when they played in Phoenix, Tucson, or the west coast. We did this for three seasons. I saw Gary smile more times on those golf courses than he had his whole time back stateside.

Music has always been a big part of Gary's life. I'd go hear him play with different country bands. He sometimes played in concert halls, but often just in a half-empty dive. When Gary stood on stage he lit up. He smiled. He laughed. With his work ethic he soon became known for precision and perfection in his performing, one of the reasons he's become a pillar of the Arizona country music scene.

While Gary is a great musician and an avid golfer, his prime post-war occupation has been as a construction superintendent. We've worked on many jobs together. As a superintendent, he is all leader, and readily whips any jobsite into shape. He's tough but fair. He's the most organized person on any jobsite. There's a ton of documentation and paperwork required for each job: plans, schedules, change orders. If you can't put your hands on certain paperwork or you miss a tiny detail along the way, you lose days and money. He told me that in Vietnam, it was ingrained in him daily that if you make a mistake you may get yourself and others killed. While the consequences aren't so severe in construction, Gary's training helped him be one of the most efficient and effective stewards of a construction project. He's one of the best in the business.

War was hell, yet that didn't end for Gary when he left the battlefield and flew home, with no one and no support waiting for him. Gary had no 'normal' left any longer so his struggle to find his post-war way shaped the man he is today. My friend is someone who is fiercely loyal and protective, unashamed to show love, happily married, a statesman of the Arizona music industry, and a champion of veterans from his and all wars. Now he is an author, sharing a story of post-combat survival in the hopes it can help others acclimate back into a stateside life they might even enjoy. But most importantly, a man anyone would be honored and fortunate to call 'friend.'

Michael Fennello

INTRODUCTION

It was another miserable, hot day in the hell they called Dong Ha, Vietnam. I was hanging on the fence just below the razor wire with my head dropped in shame. The rock I had just thrown at the POW missed, but the act stung like a killer bee. I knew instantly when he glanced towards me and our eyes met it was a cowardly act. "The Look" he gave would serve me well for the rest of my life.

We were two young men caught in a war we both knew very little about. One was being held as a trophy on display and the other just angry; waiting for his ride home from a hell hole they called war.

Who put us there does not factor. Only how we conduct the acts we are obligated to perform stands the test of time. Those acts will be memories parading through our minds for the rest of our lives causing shame, guilt, pride, or lack of either.

Within seconds after throwing that rock I knew he and I would both always remember this moment in time. The empathy overwhelming at times ends only when hopeful thoughts of his survival relieve the vision. Our path crossing again is unlikely, but that memory serves as a reminder that we will always be inseparable in thought.

This early lesson in humanity guided many actions of a nineteen year old into maturity with constant reminders. Repeating an episode of this behavior was never repeated again. So for that one look, that one look of disappointment in the prisoner's eyes I owe a deep sincere appreciation. With that split second stare I obtained a valuable necessary lesson in life.

In the Library of Congress the book of U.S. Marines in Vietnam "An Expanding War" 1966 there is mention of a prisoner captured near the Cam Lo and Dong Ha area. Under some persuasion and interrogation he gave up the plans of the Northern invaders to retake the Rock Pile and DMZ areas of Vietnam. In this little French made fort the process of extracting this information took place only one thin wall away from my presence.

Making sense of it all is the question I keep asking myself these days. We live, love, laugh, prosper, and enjoy our lives for so many years before this question even becomes a thought. In an almost panic to put it all together we may feel compelled to divide our lives in sections of importance. Remembering what made us this way, what developed our skills, and how they were acquired must shed light on where our personality and traits, good or bad, came from.

This writer hopes somehow after reading this memoir others can relate to their childhood knowing that maturity feeds the question "who am I", and how did I get this way? If we are to understand this, then it would seem possible to come to grips with our accomplishments and disappointments in a manner that will help us understand the twists and turns of your own lives.

This look back should not be to find blame, or place our find on which to blame our decisions. We were all "in charge" of our lives after a certain age. We have all had the option to change directions at any time during our adult years. Even though our childhood experiences had profound influence on our future, we all eventually knew right from wrong, and the decisions we made, good or bad, became solely our responsibility.

The potential of severe emotional toll that surfaces on most all participants is not to be taken lightly. Looking back through the years with as much detachment and humor as possible feels like a much healthier agenda.

Does denying our negative history enable us to start over, or just suggest the inability to let it go? No need, it will always be there. The primary fuel for starting this memoir has been to explore the lasting effect on combat-zone youth and military or civilian personal with similar exposure to war. I hope the following chapters will expose the intent to explain lack of accomplishments or poor choices of direction is not to lay blame on others.

It was not until after much contemplation of these memories that I came to a realization. The one single thought that kept surfacing was the miracle of my survival, not only financially, but emotionally as well. The most profound embedded memories of my survival were ones that somehow involved the Sixth Sense. Does everyone possess these qualities at the same intensity? Or is it a developed action of awareness that one cultivates? If so, then why do we not talk about it much or try to improve this 'sense'? Just as important a question is why does its power dissipate with age? Or does it? Do we all just cast its power aside in favor of more predictable schedules and agenda? Do we tend to concentrate more on logical predictability?

My feelings and dreams of astral projection were strong as a child. Many people to this day can still recall the dream state experiences. A feeling of being somewhere for the first time thinking "I know this place; I did a fly over not long ago". Have you ever taken an unfamiliar route, even though it takes longer, but smile when you reach your destination without fail? The phone rings and you instinctively know exactly who it is. This is un-charted territory for most and it's confusing to explain, but it is an ability many people possess.

There is more to the human brains capabilities than meets the eye or that the medical profession will admit exists. Near death experiences have proven to alter priorities as well as professions. The power of positive thinking and some natural elements heal. The plants on this earth which are capable of curing most health issues our race encounters are just being approved.

It must have been the "The Sixth Sense" that slammed into my body one night in Okinawa. With only days and hours before boarding the ship to Vietnam we were all encouraged to do a night in the village and enjoy ourselves. It might be sometime before the opportunity presents itself again said the platoon leader. Sleeping that suggestion off for some 12 hours after partying like a rock star I awoke.

Showered and dressed in fresh military fatigues I stepped out into the Okinawan evening darkness. Realizing the squad had managed without me for that long brought about some piece. I lay on my back in the cool grass next to the concrete barracks. On my back with thoughts racing as I gazed up at the exploding mass of stars for what must have been an hour it seemed I felt different. A feeling came over me so comforting that it produced a state of calm never before experienced.

My feet hit the Red China beach of Vietnam that early morning in 1966 and my eyes took it all in. The reality of my surroundings, the smells, the military commitment, the ugliness, and the soon to be horror of it all were clearly in view.

But in that moment, looking down at the sand, I knew without a doubt that I was going to return home safely.

A combat tour will leave you with some overwhelming memories. That's a given. How it is coped with thru the years after your return can define and control a survivor's direction. Getting professional help to mentally cope with and accept those memories will help make sense of it all.

There are now many duty stations that require a defrag regiment of help that our government has been reluctant to be responsible for in past wars. This is a good thing, but still far less than adequate by most opinions. Doing it on your own, as the majority of Vietnam vets did, was a crap shoot for most. Now that our returning combat-related vets have some level of support system in place, they must use it.

Help will not come get you. One needs to seek it out and respect the fact that even though it may seem OK now, time plays a waiting game with war memories. War, and history of war, is something we as humans must come to grips with. We may never understand the psychological reasons of this continued behavior. But for those of us who have personally experienced it, there is a way we can control our destiny after the experience.

The goal of remembering the things that have shaped our lives can become a way of dealing as well as healing after the combat tour. But we cannot forget that understanding may not stop the deep depression or anxiety. It's there and may show it's ugliness in unique forms. Learning to understand near death experiences, survival syndrome, stress, mortality and all that comes with life after combat can be therapeutically helpful.

Asking for help is not showing weakness. Our government owes it to all professional peace keepers' access to and help in healing from the physical and mental wounds obtained during service. If the agencies you are dealing with are purposely creating a "put him out to pasture" position. You should demand attention in a controlled manner that will produce results. Being persistent and professional about the personal facts will justify a positive outcome. It could be healthier moving towards promising ourselves to "survive the experience with a measure of success".

SWJ Productions

Prescott Valley, Arizona 86314

First Edition March 2015

Writing coach Trina Belanger "Quill Studios"

Front and back art works by Shakey Walls

Guidance, advice and early edit by Beve Cole

Influence and Mentor Tony Stanisci

Motivation and Tolerance Tina Cox Clemmons

ISBN: 978-1-68222-068-9

CONTENTS

ONLY CHILD & FREE

One of my earliest memories is in daycare, a word not that uncommon in today's society. A two income yielding household is almost a given in this 21st century. Back when I was a kid it seemed all of my neighborhood friends' moms were home, and living the lifestyle more common in the 50's & 60's than now.

What is best for the child at a pre school age has more than likely been publicly researched many times. If one of the parents can be home, the influences, and nurturing must yield a wide variety of good personality concepts. With that kind of early influence you would think a child might become more like the parent.

I think my childhood was awesome even though at the time it might have been considered an unfortunate situation. In the early mornings I was shuffled off to a popular professional daycare that was filled with fun, excitement, and as many types of kids as you can imagine. The teachers were aggressive in making sure there was a full day of planned activities. They functioned with the mindset that the parents were going to hear all about it. Also, if the parents could afford childcare, then the teachers better be fairly good at what they did with and for the children.

Mom had some money when we got to Phoenix, Arizona in the late 40's. She also had a great education and must have excelled in clerical work during her high school days. She had jobs with Title companies, Lawyers, and at one point was personal secretary to Frank Lloyd Wright. I remember being at his Biltmore residence occasionally on the weekends. Of course I only got the invitation if I dressed very smart, and promised to keep my manners in check the entire time. Frank was getting older then so my mom and others wrote down everything he said for future generations. Mom was fantastic at short hand to the point that she could do it with both hands at the same time when necessary.

Sometimes Mom and I would hang out by the pool with Frank at the Biltmore Hotel in Phoenix. The crystal blue water taunted me, and the smell of spicy foods we were not accustomed would linger in the air. I became just amazed at how many waitresses, and other folks would be there to communicate with us during mom's shift. Frank would always give me a quarter at the end of the day. The next week I could buy candy bars for my friends at the neighborhood store.

Independence was just a way of life for me. When I got home from school it was almost always just me. Changing from school cloths, grabbing my well broken in glove, and an extra ball, I would take off down the street to find a friend that could play. As the years rolled by the limits of my freedom were only challenged by how far I could go without getting lost.

My friends and I often found ourselves three or four miles from home at 3 in the afternoon swimming in the canals. We would find hills to ride our bikes down, or build tree forts. It seemed there were just no limits.

I can still see the sun breaking the horizon while sitting on the front porch waiting for the milkman. When he came I would say; Mom wants you to leave chocolate milk and some doughnuts. Then I would get the bounty all loaded up on the bike, and off I'd go to share my good fortune with buddies less fortunate down the street.

One day while we were swimming in the canal I cut my foot really bad on a piece of glass. The other boys didn't really know what to do as I sat there and held the ghastly looking cut together. A lady walking by said "Oh my", what have you done?" I showed her and she said let me call you a cab to take you home. With a quivering lip behind tears I told her there was no use as no one was home.

The yearning for the cool slightly green fast flowing canal water suddenly vanished. The blistering hot summer sun was baking my bare legs. The absence of breeze seemed to add to the discomfort of being stationary while waiting for the nice lady to return. She came back later with antiseptic, gauze and a bandage. We wrapped it up tight and I rode my bike home peddling with one leg. This must have been the first time I felt a little more independence than I was really comfortable with.

When I got home that afternoon, I fell asleep on the couch watching cartoons waiting for mom to get home from work. Not wanting to cause alarm, or prompt a doctor's visit to get stitches, I kept my socks on, sat around watching TV the rest of the evening and hobbled my way to bed early. As luck would have it, the wound stayed closed and healed fairly nice within a few days. That day I did learn a very effective lesson. Always wear tennis shoes when swimming in the canal. Another valuable lesson learned was how the lady showed an act of kindness during a crisis situation at the side of the canal bank.

While helping the wounded from the chopper pad to the Med Station one afternoon the young Marine looked up and caught my eye. I could see he was scared just like I had been on the side of the canal bank that day many years earlier. He saw me look at his leg with the tourniquet tied off just below the knee. I glanced over and said to the assistant corpsman" this is not that bad, you guys will fix this up in no time". Looking back into the soldier's eyes I remember saying, "You're going home Marine, You did your part".

When I was growing up surely most kids in my situation experienced a similar history of cooking and making our own meals. Being limited, to say the least, I learned how to make grilled cheese sandwiches, boil hot dogs, and heat up cans of soup. Mom kept bologna in the fridge and there was always a good supply of bread and mayo. A limited diet like that would not be a pediatrician's recommendation today, but it seemed to work just fine for me. Many years later in the jungles and primitive existence in Vietnam, eating out of a can, or making do with what you have never seemed to bother me.

Down the street living in a large house was a family that to this day remains very close to my heart. When mom and I moved to the neighborhood I couldn't wait to ride the bike down to the corner store and back. Two brothers a year apart in age made my acquaintance that day, and we hit it off right away. From that summer day on, Johnny and Gary Love became good friends. We found ourselves sharing the same experiences through life.

There were eight children under the same roof. How lucky these kids can be, I thought. Five girls and three boys actually made up a huge population of the area especially when you counted all of their friends. I was over at their place constantly. It was like a built-in babysitter for mom. She knew where I would be and counted on it daily.

The huge cottonwood tree in their back yard was our constant jungle gym until I set it on fire one day. It smoldered for at least 2 or 3 years that I can remember. Seems the fire department came out every month or so. Much later in life we all realized those drive-byes were likely to check on the pretty older Love girls and their friends. It was always a good enough reason for them to patrol, and check on the constant 14th street smoldering tree.

The Love family's father was out of their daily life just like mine. Their dad being a golf teacher and managing a driving range about 3 or 4 miles away.

Our routine most of the time was to ride the bikes to the range, jump on the golf cart, scoop up the balls, then get them washed and back into the rental bin. That would happen in the mornings and the evenings. For that we could hit all the golf balls we wanted. Sometimes we even got a soda and package of chips.

We watched their dad give swing lessons every day but we did not realize until many years later that he was one of the most popular teachers in the city of Phoenix. Every once in a while he would walk by and complain about our swing with a quick disapproving look and suggest a correction. One of my fondest memories was when the pro Weldon Love stood behind me for 3 or 4 ball launchings. Then he finally said "Let me give you a one word golf tip, Clemmons". I was excited for a brief second, until I heard him say, "Quit". Of course, he knew that would only fuel my desire even more. In fact, it could have been the very moment competitive golf became a lifelong passion. The challenge came from beating the course as well as the friends you were playing with. It is, as they say, the greatest game ever played.

As the years progressed, we had a nice way of making extra spending money. The older brother, David Love, would get us up in what seemed like the middle of the night to go Golf Ball Diving. Piling into the backseat of a '55 Chevy to be shuttled all over the valley in a 5 or 6-hour excursion of lagoon swimming was heaven. I felt like the luckiest kid on the block when, the next afternoon, I would get a couple dollars. This activity went on thru our teenage years and supported a handsome income in the summer of $20 to $30 dollars a week. Not a bad part-time job when considering the other kids were doing paper routes and mowing lawns. They were making much less, for more work, and not having near the fun.

Later in high school, I found myself deep in the hills of Oklahoma. My mom had been diagnosed with breast cancer. Those days it was a death sentence measured in months most of the time. There wasn't a golf course within a hundred miles. A young intern teacher Don Patrick came to the school one year so we became friends. He took us to neighboring towns in the late evenings on occasion. We would drive around until a golf course came into view and then we'd dive in lagoons for golf balls. We kept the golf balls and for the remainder of that school year we used them to start a golf program on the school grounds during recess. At that time, the back woods rural area of Oklahoma was most definitely not a golfer's paradise. Golf was not something that very many indulged in around those parts.

I'll rewind a little because this segment could shed some light on a personality quirk that might have developed into many lifesaving incidents in later years.

It was the summer of my 4th year of grade school when mom decided I needed to go to summer camp for 2 weeks. The vans rolled to a stop close to a wonderful town in the pines called Payson, Arizona. In front of me were a group of cabins. The long drive with kids I did not know was painful. We all stepped off the van and saw counselors greeting us with smiles and a look of anticipation behind their glasses. This bothered me as well. Ah, I thought, another group of faith-based folks poised to straighten me out for sure.

When the vans turned around to leave, it felt like my fate was sealed. Alone, helpless, and now they thought I was one of them. Oh No....I'm not! I'll show them a thing or two about tuff guys from 14th street and Indian School Rd. Phoenix.

We went to the cafeteria where lunch was served. That's when I spotted a buck knife in a corner of the speaker's podium compartment. Pretending to go use the restroom, I managed to grab the knife and slip outside the cafeteria and away from any watchful eyes. It was a very heavily wooded area with a thicket of trees when I singled out a pine with a huge trunk. I thru that knife the same way at least 15 times from different distances until it finally stuck. The knife stuck every time standing at that same distance, as the repetition set in, it was even amazing to me.

Soon, a kid my age came out and started watching. It was not long before he was impressed too. The boy ran inside to tell everybody about the knife-wielding expert. The next thing I knew I had an audience of at least 20 counselors and kids. And that knife just kept sticking every time with precision.

A short time later the lead counselor said; "Gary, one more throw then we have a schedule to keep". As I strolled to the tree to fetch the knife for that last toss, I saw a very large and brightly colorful caterpillar on the ground. So I picked it up and started showing it to everyone. Then I placed it between some loose bark on the tree about 4' high off the ground. As I silently counted my 15 steps away, turned, and took my stance, I remember thinking, "OK, Gary, just one more stick and I'll feel no more embarrassment around these people. I will command only admiration, and acceptance while earning respect for the leader I was born to be. Just rare back, and let it fly.

I did not care where it stuck, as long as it did stick. As my hand and arm started back it felt like time had slowed and suddenly an enhanced brightness surrounded the event. The knife stuck solid with a quiver and thud of hardened steel and cut that caterpillar perfectly in half. The juices of the colorful bug flew all over a couple screaming young girls. The looks on the councilor's faces as I stood there proudly was priceless. Their jaws dropped as if saying "are you kidding me". At that moment, I became the hero that everybody wanted to hang with for the next two weeks. Me, well it was going to be a wonderful 2 weeks of fun in the pines now that everyone knew who Gary Clemmons was. I know, a little full of myself at this age, but it came with the territory.

The memories we live with have shaped and led us to decisions that made us the individual who we've become. The circumstances that surrounded my childhood years allowed me to be comfortable being a loner-type personality. But, at the flip of a coin it felt natural for me to entertain people also. It seems to be something many of us are able to turn off and on at will. At parties we can often be somewhat unsociable and shy and then turn around, being center stage and feel nothing but confidence.

Some lessons learned both as a child and during combat, more than likely have helped all of us to continue to survive life's challenges. Your own personal recollections and memories will become part of your life story. And really, all any of us want more than anything is to travel through our life maintaining a comfortable level of happiness and success.

Of course being dropped into a full blown war zone at 19 years of age most certainly will shape the remainder of a young adult life. One near death experience will also most certainly change anybody. Imagine these ordeals happening on a weekly basis for an extended time over a combat tour. There will be some serious group PTSD symptoms that follow.

The Vietnam campaign plus all the battles America dealt with previously unleashed a problem demographic. It is almost inconceivable that our government's systematic refusal to deal with the participants fell on deaf ears.

From the elected officials to the private sectors neglect to expose the need is beyond comprehension.

The recollections one can remember must have shaped, and led us to decisions that made us individually who we are, and whom we've become. Some lessons learned more than likely helped all of us survive life's challenges. To maintain a degree of success traveling through life is everyone's desire.

Your own personal recollection and documentation of your memories will not only serve as a family keepsake but surly put things into perspective. This will help when, or if that midlife crisis appears, then the fruits of labor it took will all be worthwhile.

EARLY MUSICIAN

As a youngster in grade school becoming as talented a musician as my mother seemed like an un-attainable goal. She had acquired a notable level of talent out of high school playing saxophone. Her era was the very inspiring Big Band sound that, if given a listen, will still find a place in people's hearts to this day.

Her favorite "achievement story" she told friends always came with a sweet smile, and sparkle in her eyes. She had earned 1'st chair rights as a high school senior on Saxophone. That position came with the opportunity to sit-in with the hired band at the Jr. / Sr. prom close to the end of the school year.

Back in those days, it was an attainable goal for the combined classmates to save enough money to hire a class act for their prom. My mom had been thrilled to learn parts to a few songs and play with the likes of Arty Shaw or others. It was an experience she never forgot. The memory explained her lively moves along with an uncontrollable giggle whenever she listened to swing music.

By today's standards, mom had trouble with drinking. In the 50's and 60's finishing off the day over a couple of cocktails in downtown Phoenix must have been fairly routine. Especially while working for lawyers, title agencies, and as a shorthand specialist. Eventually, I become aware that during the day she managed a respected career and professional life that had respect while I spent my days in child care, and later in school. The memory of the mom I remember seemed to be a bit clumsy, clingy and, at times, childlike herself. After I became aware of what I thought should be normal behavior after a few drinks, on many occasions I would often become short, disappointed or embarrassed.

My father only visited me one time during my life. I was about 10 years old when he showed up with a baseball glove and bat. He was dressed sharp in a suit and looked refined, slim and distinguished from a military career. Just before he pulled away in the taxi that was waiting for him out front, he answered the only question I asked that day. "Do you have to go now"? He said "Yes, and as you get older you will understand why". I never saw or talked to him again after that day nor did I ever understand why. He had started another family in Tennessee so must have felt it was time to sever ties for the good of all.

Schools at that time had huge budgets for music programs. Mom wanted me to be a trumpet player. She would give a little eyelid action while talking about a horn player that seemed to be the dream of her life as a young woman. The way he played with the notes. Bending them, flirting with time intervals, and a seemingly personal style of delivery that she thought daring.

I followed her suggestion until one fatal day. It was my first real experience of major stage fright. She had arranged for me to play taps at the Eagles Hall during a veteran's service. Everything seemed to be fine until I stepped out on that big, tall stage with huge drapes and theatrical lighting above and below.

From my perspective, it looked like the entire town had shown up for my recital. You've heard of cold feet? Well, I got hot feet and ran for the back door. I dropped my trumpet, and ran like the wind for at least a half mile or so. I ran far enough away to be sure no one was following while cutting through alleyways and back yards. Later that evening when mom got home she just laid that Trumpet at the foot of my bed. When I arrived from my Little League game that evening we had a good talk. She assured me that I would never have to play the horn or take any more music lessons from that point on. I felt such relief and was reassured that mom was a darn good mom after all.

Vietnam was so damn hot. Really hot! Being an Arizona boy softened the blow for sure. While there in Vietnam I always wondered about the colder weather guys and how they managed to sustain. The ability to move around this country briskly most definitely rendered the home team advantage.

I was resting on my cot after an exhausting day in the sun, rain, mosquitoes and whatever element came along on the average day. It was sunset, almost dark outside, when an excited Lieutenant lifted the entrance to our tent. When I looked over at him it was just in time to hear his commanding voice say Clemmons". I jumped up to attention and said, "Yes Sir, I'm Clemmons. I stood there with my green fatigues bloused up at my jungle boots, and a white T-Shirt thinking "Oh Shit, what have I done this time." He said; "I've talked to your Sergeant and he said you play guitar and sing some. " I reluctantly said yes sir, I do". He said, well, grab your guitar and follow me "on the double". I reached under my bed, pulled out my least sweat stained fatigue shirt and put it on.

As we walked briskly to an area in the compound that was usually off limits to enlisted personal without permission, he began to explain. "You are going to sing a few familiar songs to the officers that are here tonight. We are throwing a little beer party to get the war off their minds. The Vietnamese band we hired can't speak, or sing a word of English."

We were soon standing at the back of a tent and I was quickly tuning the 6 rusty strings on this guitar as good as possible. "OK", the lieutenant said, you are going on right after this song is finished". We could hear some resemblance of a band playing. I heard a drummer, a horn player, and a guitar making a stab at some sort of music anyway.

The next thing I remember is being pushed under the tent flap as the officer grabbed me by the collar and guided me up to the front of the stage to the microphone. After he screamed in the microphone for about 30 seconds and got everyone's attention he said Gentlemen, please welcome Private Clemmons from 3'rd Bat., 4'th Marines. He's going to sing a few songs that, "you can understand".

The next 6 and a half seconds all I could remember was the getaway run from the Elks club 10 years prior. They didn't applaud or say a word. In that short pause all I saw was a bunch of pissed off, dirty, half tanked Marines just staring at me. I was scarred shitless! I tapped the microphone and said test a couple of times. I then hit a big E chord and started singing Kansas City with as much rhythmic enthusiasm as I could muster.

Half way through the second line of the song it sounded as though every last one of those officers broke out in loud guttural screams of approval like I've never heard in my life. They had moved forward towards the stage by this time. Colonels mixed with Captains, Full Birds and Lieutenants chanting with tears in their eyes. I let no time pass between songs as I switched to the key of A and immediately broke out in the Johnny Rivers most recent hit at the time "Madeline". It was not loud enough in that microphone. What appeared to be a seasoned soundman must have ran to the PA, because next thing you know I could hear myself again. I quickly moved between songs and then hit the familiar big chord of E one more time. This time I broke out with another song off of the latest Johnny Rivers album that I had learned back in the states, "Memphis Tennessee". The words hit home to everyone.

"Long Distance information give me Memphis Tennessee,
Help me find the Party trying to get in touch with me.

She could not leave the number, but I know the place to call"... anyway!

The beer garden tent had reached a feverish pitch of joy and excitement. When I got to the end of that song, the Lieutenant that had brought me there elbowed his way back to the stage and lifted me out of there in one big swoop as quick as he had brought me in. We couldn't stop laughing as we fell outside the rear of the tent. "That was fantastic Marine! You'll be rewarded. I'll get back with you in a day or so". In a flash I was alone again, refreshed, full of accomplishment and purpose.

It was pitch black outside as I made my way back down the rows of tents, and across the medical station to the supply area. I walked in my tent that was now so quite you could hear a pin drop. After about a half hour, my mind finally began to settle down. I remember thinking...damn if music has that kind of power, if I get out of this place, that's what I want to do for the rest of my life.

It had been just a month or so earlier that we had been on our way to Vietnam via the USS Paul Revere. It was a troop and equipment carrier with the marines stashed in the bottom of the hull. I was up on deck one afternoon and saw that a bunch of Marines were leaning over an open cargo hole applauding. It took a few minutes to work my way to the edge and look over. Down below were 3 soul brother marines snapping their fingers and singing the latest Motown hits like "My Girl" and other great songs. They were singing without accompaniment and nailing everything they did in perfect 3-part harmony. Between songs, one of them looked up the cargo hole and asked if anybody up there played guitar. Most of my company saw me board the ship with a cheap Okinawa guitar strapped to my back. The next thing I know, I'm being led 2 levels down picking up my guitar on the way. I was not that accomplished yet, but one of the guys knew when to point to the guitar at the right time and I would change chords. Needless to say I was fortunate enough to have already learned the family chords in several keys. For the next 10 days we did concerts daily. We would practice in the evenings by our bunks to the enjoyment of a different group every evening. During the day I would learn songs then perform them with my soul brother Marines in the cargo hold the next day.

Another strange turn of events that took place the weekend before heading oversees on my Vietnam tour shaped my future musical career, as well. This was our last weekend before going overseas. I had decided to stay in the barracks at Camp Pendleton outside of San Diego and just enjoy the RR of our last few days on American soil by playing pool and watching TV. The weekend before my home town had resulted in a few handshakes, a no-eye contact goodbye or two, and a couple restless, lonesome nights.

Saturday afternoon there were these three guys walking up and down the barracks saying we have one more seat left. We are going to LA for a weekend party if anyone wants to come along. I finally said, "OK, I'll go". "Well then get ready," he said, "We leave in 20 minutes. Just meet us out front of the building in the White 2-door Chevy". I put on a good set of Marine Corp dress light browns with a pressed tie and was looking sharp. When I arrived at their car they were all dressed in civilian clothes. Wow, I said... this is all I have. "That's okay, get in, and give us your share of the gas money." Fifteen dollars later we were off to LA!

The next thing I remember was pulling up to a Hollywood intersection and the driver stopped, turned around looking at me and said, "OK private, we will drop you off right here and pick you up around noon tomorrow." It caught me off guard and I said that I was under the impression we were going to do a party tonight. He just said, "Well, it's like a private affair. They might not appreciate a stranger showing up." It quickly became apparent I would become a big boy real quick so I just said, "Alright then".

Now, I'm in downtown LA for the first time in my life, and don't know a soul that lives here. I started walking around running into an entire array of hippies, bums, con artists and weirdo's. So, I had a hamburger here, and a shake there, while enjoying people staring at my uniform. I thought most folks would be respectful and show some appreciation to a serviceman. Surely, they knew I was headed over to the war to protect them from the ugly communist threat. It took until the following year before I realized that was not what 95% of those people were thinking.

It was around dusk when I walked in front of a bar; I peaked in the door and saw that it was extremely dark. There was some noise, so I lingered at the doorway for a moment. Next thing you know a voice came booming out. "Come On In, Marine"! You're here now, so you might as well start helping stock these beer coolers and pitching in with the preparation". Those were the first words of acceptance I'd heard all day. Again, the voice came from in front of me as the door slammed shut. He said, "Just stay right there for a moment, your eyes will adjust and you'll be able to see in no time.

Just as he predicted, I was starting to recognize that at least 6 girls and a few guys sweeping or wiping tables, etc. The next thing you know I'm carrying cases of beer from the cooler in the back to the front bar. I then stacked chairs, and started sweeping the floors. "Hey, this is fine, I thought, as I striped down to my white tank undershirt. Folks are talking to me. These two cute waitresses were asking me questions about when I'm going over. "This coming Tuesday morning is what we have heard", I said. They were really nice and couldn't stop telling me to be careful and make sure I come back to see them after my tour.

Two or three hours later, as the place began to take shape, I had started thinking this is either going to earn me a few bucks to get a hotel room tonight or, at least, afford me a few beers later in the evening. That was about the time I heard that big, loud booming voice again. "OK everybody hit your stations doors in 5 Minutes". The next thing I remember is that manager guy walking towards me. With a big friendly smile he said, "Get your shirt back on and follow me". We started walking up towards the stage where the big red curtain was closed. He got serious and quiet for a moment as he leaned over in my ear. He then started explaining that he had a little brother in Vietnam and how he appreciated our courage and commitment to the cause. I just said, "I'm proud to do it sir" or something like that. He then said "I want you to sit right here tonight and enjoy yourself. I'm going to keep a tab on this table tonight. You're not going to be paying for it at the end of the evening, you got that?" It was a small little table for 3, right in front of the stage. I noticed he went to the front door man and whispered a few things while pointing at me a couple times.

Soon the doors opened, and people started piling in as fast as the doorman could take their money. The place was filling up quickly. I was sitting there alone until a bouncer walked two of the prettiest girls I had ever seen in my life up to the table. He then winked at me "here you go ladies, have fun". They had no problem starting a conversation. Where are you from? When are you leaving? Where are you staying tonight? Those were about the last questions I remember answering before the third round of drinks arrived at the table. As the curtains opened they both gave me a kiss on my cheeks and said, "Well, young man, you are staying with us tonight!"

Since I was in the center seat at the time, all I had to do was look up when the curtains opened. It was a single artist playing the best rhythm guitar beat with the most incredible sound I had ever heard. The song was Memphis Tennessee and it was up close, personal, and in person with Johnny River's right there in front of me! This guy had just had an amazing record released. He was a recording star, a talent of major accomplishment. Every song took me to another level of appreciation. When his set was over, I thought the audience applause was somewhat reserved. I then heard the phrase over the speakers, "OK, we will take a short intermission and be right back." This is great I thought, more to come".

After much more dialogue and flirting with these two beauties during the intermission the curtains separated again. In full force glory came the Motown sound of the original Temptations. I was no less than completely blown away. I became pinned to the seat with amazement. They went through a set of incredible music while I tried to memorize each chord change of their hands from the musicians. The drummer was so exact and never seemed in the way, and he never lost focus of being the pulse of the band.

When the show was over we drifted outside to the flashing bright lights of wonderful, downtown Hollywood. The girls had me by each arm and guided me to their parked car. We then drove to the cutest little apartment only a few blocks away. The three of us never left each other's side for the rest of the night and morning. Many times I have wondered why an event of this kind would materialize at precisely the right time in life. A memory I will never forget is certain.

Morning came with the sweet smell of bacon and coffee behind a throbbing headache. After a couple aspirin, another shower, and some food, I mentioned that I forgot to thank the manager of the club for his generosity and kindness the night before. The ever-smiling one just said, "Oh, I will tell him for you. My brother has been working at the Whiskey A Go Go for a long time. He was proud and excited to have you in the audience last night."

Those beauties soon disappeared as quickly as they had arrived the night before. It took me many years to realize the importance that club has had on the music industry. I gathered my thoughts and started walking down the hill. The girls told me that when I got to the stop light the club would be close. I had not reached the intersection more than 2 minutes before that familiar Chevy from the afternoon before rolled up next to me. One of the Marines stuck his head out the window and said, "Hop in private. We are headed back to Camp Pendleton now".

I piled in the back seat and we headed south. They started asking me if I had a good time on the strip. Of course, I couldn't wipe the smile off my face long enough to say anything. With the window down and a sea breeze blowing in my face, we began putting the miles behind us from my first ever trip to Los Angles. I heard enough of their exploits through a half open ear on the way back to arrive at the conclusion that it had been me that had the time of my life the night before. This weekend event would fuel, and shape my motivation for many years to come. I remember thinking that night music would be my direction when I returned home. But first I had to get Vietnam behind me.

Some might say, ha! This is almost too good to be true. Not so, this chapter like all the others is as much non-fiction as my lifetime of memories will allow.

HUE, BAR TENDING

It was just before the rush hour 12:00 noon to 3:00pm at the makeshift bar erected in the compound at Hue, Phu-Bi Vietnam in 1966. I borrowed a tropical short sleeve shirt and scrounged up a starched pair of fatigues. The fresh polish on my combat boots added a nice touch as well. The beer on ice chilling down, and all the liquor bottles were wiped clean. Those fancy whiskey labels all so neatly facing the soon to enter officers of the 4th Marine Division.

Three or four weeks earlier I had entertained these same officers at a beer garden by singing a few songs. The promise of a reward was kept by assigning me 3 days duty as bar tender. It was the calm before a storm while leaning on the plywood bar recalling how just a few months earlier life was so innocent.

It was recently in the hills of Oklahoma as a senior in high school where times were so different. At 42 years old mom had been diagnosed with breast cancer. In those days it was experimental procedure more than successful treatment methods. Mom had asked a friend of hers if she would take me in during this illness. It would afford me the opportunity of getting a decent High school education.

My Grandpa from Mill Valley, California dropped a small check in the mail every month to help curb the expense. Buck & Teddy Mattox both had children from previous marriages. None of their children lived with them during my 3 years with my new guardian parents. It worked out well for me in the back hills of Oklahoma. The raising of coon dogs, a few hogs, hauling hay, picking snap beans, strawberries, and okra, gave me responsibilities. I did most of the choirs as standard duty while they worked hard long hours every day. Teddy was a nurse at the hospital, and Buck was a mechanic at the local Ford dealership in Stilwell Oklahoma.

Buck had been raised just outside of Stillwell in a small community. If I remember correctly the entire school of 1st through 12th grades comprised of only 412 student's total. The Cave Springs School had relics of rock buildings and old growth tall trees spread over about a 20 acre fenced partial. They did not leave the gym doors open during school hours. I soon assumed the smell of sweat, and jock straps filtering through the building must have been the reason. The odor would linger ever presently up and down the halls like a pungent nuisance when that hours PE segment was over. The halls were lined with past graduating classes like trophies of success. At least half of the classes were always filled with traditional Cherokee sir names. Of course to me the names always seem to describe their personalities a little more than the bloodlines. Moses, Owl, and Tenkiller, to name a few.

It was an area filled with folks that enjoyed music. It caught me off guard when a classmate asked, "What instrument do you play?" My first silent thought was how you knew I played music. I said guitar, then followed up with a statement "Why do you ask". His response was that everybody either plays or sings from these parts. OK was my thought, I'm just a little closer to acceptance.

As it turned out Dayne Dudley was the son of the school principal. We became the best of friends and it was ultimately that family who gave me such an incentive to excel in school during those learning years. Dayne played the drums so we made a mixture of country and rock music while doing gigs with my stepfather in the surrounding towns.

Dayne would help me study our class assignments as we listened to the St. Louis Cardinals night games on the radio. This routine would transpose us to the big city. The big city of St. Louis would broadcast the games to us in stunning radio black and white. We are way out here in the middle of nowhere in Oklahoma. The power of Radio and its signal would soon spark a desire. The possibility of someday working in radio shaped the entertainment thirst brewing in my soul. How ironic that people come along in one's lives that are desperately needed at just the right time.

Back in Vietnam the flimsy screen doors of the Officers Bar hooch swung open and jolted me back to reality. It was just past noon and thirsty Marines were ready to numb their minds with some relief in the form of alcohol. I took orders well and remembered the special operations officer telling me to just pay attention and don't talk much. He assured me during the crash course in drinkology there were only a few cocktails I needed to know how to make. Bourbon & Coke, Gin & Tonic, Screwdriver's, and a Bloody Mary were the main four. Any other orders, just ask them how they would like that made.

During that first days shift not one officer mentioned or asked if I were the musically talented Marine that entertained them a few weeks back. That makeshift concert venue earlier in the field tent close to the perimeter outpost seemed to have never happened. The reality of this put things in perspective fairly abruptly. The Officers hooch bar just kept getting busier, as the conversations and foul language got louder. When the next higher-ranking officer arrived thru the slamming screen door, the chorus of chitchats mellowed briefly, and then uniformly increased again.

I just kept the drinks pouring and restocking the beer on ice as best I could. Sometime close to 5 pm it got quite as fast as it filled up earlier. About that time the energetic officer arrived with another enlisted Marine. He said OK, this is your shift replacement; start tomorrow the same time as you did today. I overheard many conversations during that 3-day assignment. It's apparent that everyone was as anxious as me to get the hell out of this hellhole of a country. Get back to American girl round eyes, and Rock & Roll or their favorite kind of music.

The atmosphere was always tense in combat. It was that awkward time when America had committed to the conflict without ever determining a direction, or actual legitimate reason to be there. Our media fed the public back home what sounded like a reason, but it never really digested with the public. I bet this sounds a little familiar.

Vietnam was under my boots and I had better get this survival thing figured out quickly. Third Battalion of the 4th Marines is now committed to a town forty-five miles north of Da Nang near Hue. Phu Bai is where I landed in February or March of 1966, and I'll be damned if I'm going to die in this foreign land.

I remember thinking after that first days bar tending duty. If this was a reward it just might be better to distribute C rations, water cans, and carry ammo supplies to the squads in the bush all day long. That notion dissipated soon even though I did get two more days of bar tending before continuing my assigned duties.

A supply grunt in a combat zone is not exempt from any kind of duty what so ever. The days remaining at Hue before relocating up North to Dong Ha, and Cam Lo by the DMZ were filled with convoys to front line positions. We manned foxholes in front of 5-5-howitzer canon positions. We walked many patrols on the outskirts of small villages around the neighborhoods. This became regular events for the company as searching out enemy supply stash positions were a necessity.

It wasn't much later when my bar tending position was just a memory as we relocated to Cam Lo. This Marine post was further up the coast towards the

DMZ. This was as about as close as you could get to North Vietnam with more committed ground objectives. Getting a couple of hot beers once in a while soon did not seem like much reward or relief.

I was spreading new socks, ammo, poncho's and gear one afternoon when the chatter was about not everyone getting a ration of Beer like the officers got. Of course I made the statement that I could get them some beer. When the dinner hour was wrapping up I went searching for a jeep to borrow. Of course I was not going to ask for one, just use it for a short time. A short distance from my area was this tent with 4 or 5 small jeeps parked. I looked in all of them until the shiny keys in one just seemed to say, "Pick-me".

Earlier I had noticed a staging location for food and supplies over by the air-strip. When I stopped behind the opened flaps of a row of tents I grabbed a clipboard from the center by the seat. Sure enough it did not take long to find the pallets of nice warm Beer. A lower ranking enlisted man saw me loading up cases in the jeep, and came over to ask what I was doing. Grabbing the clip board I said I was filling an order for the Major. He looked at the jeep and said OK carry on.

That's when I realized the jeep did look new, and seemed to have some important things in the back seat as well. I returned to the Marine area using a not so conventional route sensing folks might be a little pissed off that their jeep was not parked where they left it. I unloaded the beer a few tents away from the nightly poker game tent. Covered them up nicely and parked the Jeep a few 100 yards away. When I returned to my area the first thing I did was tell the Marines around me that if anybody asked, I have not left the supply tent all afternoon. My hunch was correct! Some very agitated Lieutenants stormed into the hooch in about 5 minutes. They looked right at me and asked where I had been. My poker face and confused eyebrows sold the program. I said No Where, Why? They looked at the other two Marines in my tent and asked them if I had been gone recently. Both of them knew I had the beer stashed and was not about to sell me out.

It was later information around the camp that someone had stolen some beer from the Air Force staging area down by the airstrip. Not only that, but they took a joy ride in the Major's jeep. He had to hitch a ride back to his unit until his wheels showed up sometime later.

As it turned out that was only the beginning of a weird and dangerous night of activity on my part. I started the poker game by lantern light around 8:00pm as normal, and most of the usual faces showed up. I had managed to find some ice as well so there was a stash of cold beer for the players that evening.

I was getting fairly wasted as we had plenty of booze. That combination and one of the poker players not really knowing the rules of the game sparked a heated argument that only lasted about 2 minutes. It involved a huge pot of money that had been wagered that hand. I had a flush, someone had a straight, and one Marine had 3 of a kind as we showed our hole cards. The guy with the straight started raking the money uncontested. He was a huge ole boy and most definitely toasted to put it mildly. No one wanted to dispute the fact that he had not won that hand; in fact it was I who had the winning hand of a flush. That's when I took things to another level.

Within reaching distance behind me was my ammo belt. In one swift motion I grabbed a grenade, pulled the pin and slammed it down in the middle of the poker table. I was holding the grenade in place firmly when I saw the whites of everyone's eyes very clearly. I said look, a flush beats a straight OK..... Now when I let go of this lever we all have about 4 seconds to either get the hell out of the way or get blown up. You over there holding my money.....I'm going to toss it at you if you start running.

Before I could get the words completely out all the Marines around the table were trying to assure him that yes I was correct, a flush beats his little straight. The whites of his eyes dominated the sockets that held them. A sobering stare of a few seconds must have convinced him to pay attention.

The big intercity bully, with the intimidating demeanor, un-educated in the poker field Marine just smiled real big and said OK I understand. Here is your money, settle down now, and put that pin back in.

Well it would not go back in. I explained the game was over for the evening and they all said that was fine. Now all by myself I noticed the knuckles on my right hand were starting to turn white after I stashed all the money in my pockets. I've got my other hand holding the grenade as well while I walked over to the ordinance tent.

The look of me coming in with the grenade in my hand and explaining the pin had been removed demanded immediate attention as one can imagine. They wrapped my hand up very tightly before finding a pin to replace the one I had pulled. When things settled down a small inquiry was being held in my honor. I just told them I was rearranging my ammo belt and it accidentally came out. The explanation seemed to be enough for the time being.

History will state that when I got to Vietnam there were about 50,000 troops in country. By the time I rotated back to America we were somewhere close to having about 350,000 troops in a campaign that was never declared an actual war. In a few short years after I went home we had sent about a half of million to this foreign country. That's a lot of commitment to a country that really never wanted us over there in the first place.

When I landed at Edwards Air Force base upon my return from combat the ugliness of war arrived with me. In December of 1966 a nightly newscast shows a demonstration of students at the University of California Berkeley. In fact many protests were springing up daily. While in Vietnam this was all kept under hat. On occasion when a replacement troop would filter into your unit they would make small talk of unsettling events back in the states.

I still had about 2 and a half years left in the military. My 4-year enlistment needed to stay true. I believed in my Marine Corps, and the promise of health care, a home loan, and a future educational benefit. With those needs weighing heavily I kept my opinions quite. While duty stations at Camp Pendleton, Charleston S.C., and Quantico Va. were in my future I'm sure glad I did.

The immediate years upon returning PTSD was not a sickness anybody wanted to admit. It felt weak and made to seem not adult. I do not know the exact numbers or percentage of combat vets that needed desperate help. I can relay some other ridicules examples of screaming out for help that I was experiencing. Facing the need for help is not weakness, its survival with dignity and quality of life.

While on weekend leave in Phoenix my hometown around early 1967 I was a mess. Of course that is even putting it mildly. We had a very popular hamburger chain called Bob's Big Boy downtown. After another night of complete rejection by most I came into contact with I barely survived an ugly episode.

The place was jam packed so since I was by myself a seat at the counter was available. Still being in the service my short hair was a giveaway during that era. I felt complete rejection and avoidance after a short wait. That's when it felt appropriate to stand up and start throwing the sugar, salt, pepper, water glass, and anything I could reach against the wall. It must have been a menacing site as the fear on the patrons faces occasionally came into focus.

These types of incidents started to become more frequent. They were also more aggressive as the months wore on. Hearing the nightly news, projecting myself back to the war zone, and pure exhaustion from lack of sleep would anger me with alarming consistency.

Scrambling back to the base after a weekend leave with feelings of shame and confusion were common. There were no follow up appointments at sick bay to check our mental status. If a Sargent or commanding officer noticed a change in your demeanor then a transfer seemed to cure their concerns.

I eventually started learning how to control my anger on the outside anyway. Deep within still lurks the horror of combat duty. Sure the near death experiences would surface less often. The shame of every unjust deed in the war zone that hit the nightly news layered on top of this already fractured shell.

When my 4 year enlisted obligation was over I scrambled out of the military in full stride. I must now be ready to correct the interruption of normality with gusto. Many that took my path may relate to how we coped after the war. Indulging very deeply into work was the way to quite the mind. Jobs, and part time jobs were needed to keep driving forward to make up for lost time. This action had a by-product called divorce, anger, and be in control or die.

Sacrificing the normal process of growth in the social realm is another lasting problem for many after combat. High school, adolescent, and even preteen exposure to sex was common place in my neighborhood growing up. It was the feeling of abandonment by our country that later drove many combat veterans into a seclusion or artificial acceptance by the opposite sex.

My need to be in control or die contributed heavily to 3 divorces and reluctance to nurture many relationships. Do all things really happen for a reason? Sure we have to look at it that way because there is no way of judging a future that did not happen.

Of course war got in the way of a participants normal growth pattern as it does in every generation since time began. So there you go, it's not so abnormal after all. We are not victims, only students of survival.

One of my very close civilian friends just told me, remember we used to call you Sarg all the time. Then he followed up with, it is so good to see you have mellowed over the years. I just wanted to ask him how he hung on as a friend all these years. The fact that we are still good friends is a testament to his understanding who I was, and looking beyond the surface of my outer self.

My actions at times must have been that of a mad scientist trying to discover a magical formula to not only financial but personal success and respect. I answered my own question upon driving away that day. It was the mission as well as the desire to survive the combat ordeal. It became a necessity to not let the war define you. Face it, the Vietnam War will always be part of you in memory and the future. There was a popular phrase in a recent movie I started using as a motto. "If you're not dying then let's get busy living". I've been pleasantly surprised of how at peace with myself I have become.

WOUNDED AT THE CHOPPER PAD

"Oh yes, I'll be back, we are in a hell of a fight up there" were the words of the gunner just before he jumped back on the chopper. A lift off with a blast of down draft had us ducking and holding our helmets. He hit the throttle with the authority of a man that knew his bird. Only his toy can produce the adrenaline it takes to command his spirit.

It was a hot summer day in 1966 when the war came to my front door. Things started off fairly normal that morning as our company loaded up and headed North to the DMZ area from Cam Lo. We were holding down the Headquarters Company position. I had just issued the troops some last minute jungle gear and a few of the Marine Corps standard canvas covered boots. Things settled down for a couple hours and I kept the supply hooch in a resemblance of order.

It was close to noon when a young Captain came to me very calm. He was a surgeon or something that I'd seen many times working just a few yards away in the "B" Med Station. He asked me to get over to the Chopper landing area on the other side of the hospital tent so I could help with the arriving wounded. I closed the doors on the old French Fort being used to stash supplies, grabbed my M-14, and started the brisk walk.

I arrived at the chopper pad just in time to feel the tremendous down draft of wind the approaching helicopter was churning up. There was a litter on either side of the gunner's open doors, plus at least one more casualty inside. Two of us took off in a running stance and went to the further side of the Huey and snatched the stretcher from the runners. We worked our way around to the waiting jeeps. There were at least 3 corpsmen, a few doctors and drivers that were working in unison to secure the wounded for the short transport to the medical station tents. It took awhile to prep them for delivery. During that time the wounds were partially visible. So was the smoke rising from their burning smoldering bodies.

There must have been the fading sound of the choppers as they banked back towards the North but the memories of those and other sounds have faded. The sound most assuredly in memory came from the agony of the wounded. Also were the shouted orders from the assembled team. Those and other sounds have mostly faded but the visual memory and the smell of human flesh burning is something that never leaves. After a few more choppers brought in more wounded it all became routine. There would be some dialogue in the hours to follow, but never anything personal. Our obvious questions were never answered. Questions like how these wounded were getting burned and what was going on up there? Listening to the nightly newscasts when I was back in the states were reports suggesting our own napalm as the likely source.

The sunset and quiet skies confirmed that the immediate situation was at hand. All the extra help summoned drifted back to their assigned duties. The sounds and smells of food around the compound slowly took over the evening hours. I was 19 years of age and that day I had come face to face with the reality of war. It was a night many would truly be looking forward to the 2 hot beers if we could get them. Then I would write a letter home to help take the sting out of this day's activities.

Emergency amputations and operations were taking place in the Med Station. The field hospital that was silhouetted against the moonlight appeared fictional.

I drifted over when the activity seemed to peak just to see if I could be of some assistance. Sheets were hanging everywhere. They had the space divided into 6 or 8 uniform cubicles that still held the wounded. The biggest commotion came from one corner of the tent so I worked my way over without being questioned. I was a bit surprised to see all of the hospital staff watching a movie and chirping words of approval at suggestive dialogue. I tried to join them in their playful mood with no success. Soon I was finding my way back to my sleeping tent feeling a bit disturbed and confused.

It took years of that footage rolling through my memory before I realized it must have been a stress release ritual combat medics engage in as needed. It also took until the third time watching reruns of the series Mash for me to appreciate the experience. The humor and joke playing seen in Mash was not a portrayal of any combat zone field hospital I remembered.

Without ever really being tutored or trained in the art of being a supply man, I took to the job with precision. Platoon leaders, young Lieutenants, grunts, cooks, and administrative men would ask for things. When I did not have them my mind would start figuring out how to get them. This brought on a scavenger mentality as time progressed during my 13 month tour. I learned how to negotiate around the compound without bringing too much attention to the tasks brought before me. I used the many years of wheeling and dealing around my neighborhood as a youngster to serve me in combat several times.

One time during the summer between 5th and 6th grades my friends and I took a couple of firecrackers from the Phoenix Country Club golf course the night the 4th of July fireworks show was under way. Initially we had climbed over the fence headed for the lagoon to get golf balls. We crawled on from bush to bush on our bellies hiding from the spotters on lawn maintenance equipment watching the show. It only took us a short time to learn the routine of the experts lighting the fuses of the high rising fireworks show.

We waited using hand signals until the perfect moment. Like experienced Navy Seals or Recon troops we dove for the stash of firecrackers at just the right moment. Then we scrambled back to cover without detection. When we realized the heist was successful we couldn't hold back an attack of laughter. We lay in the darkness under the brush beside one of the beautiful fairways of the Phoenix Country Club recapping the precision of our execution.

We only waited a couple of nights before an exciting plan developed. I'm sure my input held some weight when deciding what to do with bombs. This was by no means the first attempts to entertain my neighborhood group.

Our grade school grounds had 4 baseball diamonds. We were surrounded by a large sub-division of houses. Just off to the East of the school grounds stood the Baptist church I had attended many Sunday mornings. The plants, shrubbery and grassy lawn served as the perfect place to launch the highflying projectile. It would go over the fence and high above the organized little league games that were under way that perfect summer evening.

We had no way of knowing what type of firecracker it was, but hoped it was a colorful display of Red, White, & Blue to awe the sports teams and attending families a couple hundred yards away. The earth was hard to dig in so the tube we had acquired never really got buried deep enough. Our nervous energy took over as launch time was announced. One of us was holding the tube at just the correct angle as another lit the fuse. When the projectile came roaring out of the tube it shook so hard it forced the holder to move off the intended angle. The firecracker flew low and landed in the middle of the ball fields. Only a couple center fielders saw it coming and moved out of the way. When it exploded there were no colorful sulfur pods. It was only this blood-curdling bang that shook the entire neighborhood. You could feel the air move in waves. It was enough sound to resemble a cluster of lightning strikes happening all at the same time.

We all lived in this neighborhood so we knew every oleander, back yard and irrigation ditch available. I remember yelling, "Split up", and "don't get caught". We knew that the police might start patrolling the area looking for the "hoodlums". I had only gotten about half way home when I noticed the neighborhood was swarming with patrol cars. Fortunately, we all made it back to our homes without detection. The next morning bright and early we all found ourselves under a familiar palm tree by the ball field laughing like crazy. I don't remember for sure but I'll bet we soon grabbed our best ole patched up tire tubes and headed for the canal for a float.

Snooping around camp at night in a war zone is not an easy task or a smart thing to do. It was just necessary to shop for extra beer, food, and specialty items from the different branches of service around the air base. When I pulled guard duty on the perimeter, many childhood experiences served me well.

There was a Sergeant sent to the company who only spent a few weeks at best with us. He could not sleep and was a mess the night I came across him. I could never just hang out in the foxhole during my watch so I often snooped around with a keen eye towards the perimeter wire. It was very early in the morning and I was alert watching the supply tents from all angles. The sleeping areas were all quiet and dark as I came around the outside of the Non-Commissioned Officers tent.

Just in front of me was the backside of this huge Marine. I stood there for the longest time evaluating whether or not he had a rifle or pistol at the ready before creeping up on him very slowly. He was only smoking and looking very intently to the bush. I began to speak soft and controlled in normal voice. "What are you doing up so early this morning Sir?"

It was obvious to see he was very scared and that I had startled him. He started to reprimand me about sneaking up on him. When I found an opening I reminded him I was on guard duty and it was my job to keep an eye on things during these early morning hours. He paused, then agreed and continues to tell me he hears something in the bush just out there a ways. Trying to put him at ease I told him I would check on it.

I cautiously headed out from the compound about 50 yards towards the direction he had pointed. From that vantage point I could see the stock pond and rice paddy the local village folks used for irrigation and water buffalo. I kept an eye and ear out for some time. Every so often he would whisper in a loud hiss, "Do you hear it? Can't you hear it?" I would never answer him because I did not want my position compromised.

Not long afterwards I heard what sounded like a motorized vehicle getting a little louder with each breath I took. I got down very low and checked my weapon. The moon was semi-bright when the American tank came into view. The engine unmistakably working its way thru the muddy jungle floor started getting louder. It traveled directly through the rain-flooded grounds coming right at me. When the point man was in hearing range just in front of me, I yelled out, "Halt and state your purpose". The Marine said, "Hold your fire sentry we are coming in from a night recon assignment." Hearing the perfect English I relaxed and they proceeded around our compound to an area of artillery and tank battalions.

I worked my way back to the Sergeant and explained that one of our motorized night patrols was late and a little off course, but things were all secure. He looked like he was on the verge of tears and just about ready to have a nervous breakdown. A day or two later I hiked over to his area looking for him. The Gunnery Sgt. I spoke with said they shipped him back to Okinawa. I just assumed he could not take the pressure and was not suited for the duty assignment.

The years spent around the Country Clubs "at night" snooping around the golf courses seemed to be paying off in a combat zone at night. Many years prior learning quickly as the night watchmen and greens keepers knew all the tricks. They were experienced on how to watch for suspected lagoon diving, golf ball getting heathens. Timing was everything, observation was essential to learn each course's routine. If we did get caught they would never do anything except escort us from the property anyway. In the combat zone I knew the difference, it's for keeps now. But at least it was a familiar substance of awareness.

Just five years before I was sent to Vietnam, we were in Phoenix becoming experienced at avoiding detection. Now in combat knowing what to watch for around the waterways as the night arrived was a valuable, possibly lifesaving lesson. The relief of surviving each situation while we all counted off our remaining days in theater was the greatest payoff.

After a beachhead landing 3rd Bat. 4th Mar. Camp in Phu-Bi, VN. 1'st day Early 1966

Outside Hue, VN supply tents are pitched and ready for business with 3'rd Bat. 4th Marines

Just enough time to snap a couple photo's going out on our 1'st operation from Phu-bi, VN

At boot camp graduation San Diego MCRD with mom in late 1965

A week into base camp came the local kids looking for laundry or housekeeping work.

Nightly perimeter positions had to be assigned for protection.

Hygiene was sparse but necessary. Shower call from 5 gallon water can's.

Our Battalions 1'st operation loading into the 6X trucks for speedy sector assignments.

6X trucks were loaded and troops delivered to recon information of enemy locations.

2-man teams were assigned, but somehow names were not something you remembered.

The operations I became personally involved in at some capacity during my tour.

1. LAST NAME—FIRST NAME—MIDDLE NAME		2. SERVICE NUMBER	3. SOCIAL SECURITY NUMBER
CLEMMONS, Gary Lynn		214 45 96	▇▇ ▇▇ ▇▇

4. DEPARTMENT, COMPONENT AND BRANCH OR CLASS		5a. GRADE, RATE OR RANK	5b. PAY GRADE	6. DATE OF RANK	DAY	MONTH	YEAR
USMC		Sgt	E-5		01	Apr	69

7. U.S. CITIZEN	8. PLACE OF BIRTH (City and State or Country)	9. DATE OF BIRTH	DAY	MONTH	YEAR
☒ YES ☐ NO	Sioux Falls, South Dakota		05	Nov	46

10a. SELECTIVE SERVICE NUMBER	10b. SELECTIVE SERVICE LOCAL BOARD NUMBER, CITY, COUNTY, STATE AND ZIP CODE	10c. DATE INDUCTED	DAY	MONTH	YEAR
Not Available	Not Available			N/A	

11a. TYPE OF TRANSFER OR DISCHARGE			11b. STATION OR INSTALLATION AT WHICH EFFECTED
Transferred to Marine Corps Reserve			Hq, ServBn, MCB, QUANT

11c. REASON AND AUTHORITY 210-Convenience of the Government, Paragraph 6012.14 MARCORSSEPMAN & MCO 1900.2F	11d. EFFECTIVE DATE	DAY	MONTH	YEAR
		29	May	69

12. LAST DUTY ASSIGNMENT AND MAJOR COMMAND	13a. CHARACTER OF SERVICE	13b. TYPE OF CERTIFICATE ISSUED
ServCo, ServBn, MCB, QUANT	HONORABLE	N/A

14. DISTRICT, AREA COMMAND OR CORPS TO WHICH RESERVIST TRANSFERRED	15. REENLISTMENT CODE
Marine Corps Automated Service Center, Kansas City, Missouri	RE-1

16. TERMINAL DATE OF RESERVE/UNITS OBLIGATION			17. CURRENT ACTIVE SERVICE OTHER THAN BY INDUCTION a. SOURCE OF ENTRY		18. TERM OF SERVICE	c. DATE OF ENTRY		
DAY	MONTH	YEAR	☒ ENLISTED (First Enlistment) ☐ ENLISTED (Prior Service)			DAY	MONTH	YEAR
17	May	71	☐ OTHER ☐ REENLISTED	b. CURRENT ACTIVE SVC	04(a)	01	Jun	65

19. PRIOR REGULAR ENLISTMENTS	19. GRADE, RATE OR RANK AT TIME OF ENTRY INTO CURRENT ACTIVE SVC	20. PLACE OF ENTRY INTO CURRENT ACTIVE SERVICE (City and State)
None	Pvt (E-1)	Little Rock, Arkansas

21. HOME OF RECORD AT TIME OF ENTRY INTO ACTIVE SERVICE (Street, RFD, City, County, State and ZIP Code)	22.	STATEMENT OF SERVICE	YEARS	MONTHS	DAYS
Route #1 Stilwell, Adair, Oklahoma 74960	a. CREDITABLE FOR BASIC PAY PURPOSES	(1) NET SERVICE THIS PERIOD	03	11	29
		(2) OTHER SERVICE	00	00	14
23a. SPECIALTY NUMBER & TITLE	23b. RELATED CIVILIAN OCCUPATION AND D.O.T. NUMBER 909.137	(3) TOTAL (Line (1) plus Line (2))	04	00	13
3051-Cashierman		b. TOTAL ACTIVE SERVICE	03	11	29
	Warehouse Foreman	c. FOREIGN AND/OR SEA SERVICE	01	01	06

24. DECORATIONS, MEDALS, BADGES, COMMENDATIONS, CITATIONS AND CAMPAIGN RIBBONS AWARDED OR AUTHORIZED
Presidential Unit Citation   Vietnam Service Medal w/2*
Good Conduct Medal (1st Award)   Vietnam Campaign Medal w/device
National Defense Service Medal   Rifle Sharpshooter Badge

25. EDUCATION AND TRAINING COMPLETED
High School - 4 years - Academic

26a. NON-PAY PERIODS/TIME LOST (Preceding Two Years)	b. DAYS ACCRUED LEAVE PAID	27a. INSURANCE IN FORCE (NSLI or USGLI)	b. AMOUNT OF ALLOTMENT	c. MONTH ALLOTMENT DISCONTINUED
None	15 days	☐ YES ☒ NO	$ N/A	N/A
	28. VA CLAIM NUMBER c. N/A	29. SERVICEMEN'S GROUP LIFE INSURANCE COVERAGE ☒ $10,000 ☐ $5,000 ☐ NONE		

30. REMARKS
Good Conduct Medal Period commences: 1Jun66 (2nd Award)

31. PERMANENT ADDRESS FOR MAILING PURPOSES AFTER TRANSFER OR DISCHARGE (Street, RFD, City, County, State and ZIP Code)	32. SIGNATURE OF PERSON BEING TRANSFERRED OR DISCHARGED
See Block #21	

33. TYPED NAME, GRADE AND TITLE OF AUTHORIZING OFFICER	34. SIGNATURE OF OFFICER AUTHORIZED TO SIGN
F. E. DAUBENSPECK, Captain, Bn ExecO	

DD FORM 214 MC (1900) 1 JUL 66   PREVIOUS EDITIONS OF ARMED FORCES OF THE UNITED STATES THIS FORM ARE OBSOLETE   REPORT OF TRANSFER OR DISCHARGE   S-N 0102-002-0000   MARINE CORPS DISTRICT-7

Rank at discharge and citation awards information from service record book

After playing a few songs for the officers in the war zone I got bar tending duty for 3 days

Just before shipping over to Vietnam my spare time spent with the enlisted band in Okinawa

Just prior to relocating from Phu-Bi to Dong Ha up North in I-corps, some time for a guitar lesson.

Once a day local kids came begging for C-rations or housekeeping chores.

Just before discharge at Quantico, Va. Very proud to have served.

Guard duty at Charleston S.C. Naval base on main gate duty.

奇跡の神

Vietnam propaganda leaflet.

Iwo Statue in Washington D.C. 2011, 8th & I barracks parade field.

TRIP WIRE ON A PANT LEG

In Marine Corp boot camp they taught us how to set a claymore land mine. This anti-personnel device received at least one classroom lesson, and one field set up training procedure. When it became time to actually implement this in a combat setting the realizations of possible disaster became very apparent.

Just outside of Hue, Phu-Bi, Vietnam I found myself in a nighttime operation to protect the 105 howitzer positions that were pounding the hillsides to the west. We were a convoy of four or five trucks headed out around noon one tropical March day. I was on top of supplies aboard a troop truck headed to a place where it was evidently not necessary to inform the enlisted men of the exact agenda. The assignment was discussed only in real time, or as it was happening.

We were traveling 30 or 40 miles per hour on a narrow dirt road watching the waving Vietnamese kids beg for C rations. The billowing red dirt that looked like chili powder rolled up from the tires in front of us. It seemed to always keep a thick haze of dust surrounding the convoy. Cases of personal food rations were individually boxed. The dates on the canned foods read like a history lesson from the early 40's. These rations of food were packed on top of a full bottom row of 5-gallon water cans. I was sitting up high observing the roadside children gathered in packs with their arms out as we recklessly drove by within inches of their out reaching hands and sad eyes.

Most of the time while passing at 40 mph it was within only a foot or so from their tiny little human frames. After time in country it becomes obvious that the kids begging were good at it. It seemed like a phase of their life giving back to their village and families. The parents did it during the French occupation 10 or 15 years prior. The grownups always ran to the back as we passed, anticipating a case of food being dropped off the tailgate. Momma-san or grandpa-san seemed to always be thirty or forty yards away. They relaxed in their common position of squatting while chewing their beetle nut leaves. We sensed they were only frozen in observation ready to run interference and fairness when the booty was delivered. I always assumed the entire village reaped the benefits if any were given.

I remember thinking how could these C-rations be any good? They were prepared during World War II. It seems we never looked at dates when we were hungry. The variety was just enough to be interesting. So the mix and match possibilities were always being tested to the fullest by the various ethnic groups represented in our America military.

When we reached our destination of the big gun positions I quickly surveyed the area. They were Marines all right; you could see it in their eyes. They had no shirts on as if to say, "It's just too hot to stay dressed". The controlled arrogance about their demeanor was present. They were bulked-up, with brown tanned bodies, all staging shells in preparation. The order to man the guns and direct fire at the call of the radioman close by seemed a powerful tool of war. A few of us spent the next couple of hours spreading out the supplies behind the big guns. Each location got about six 5-gallon cans of water and about that many cases of C-rations. We had Sundry packages ready with cigarettes and candy that we placed on top of their rations.

Each battery of personal manning the guns was very appreciative and friendly towards us. It was not until one of them said we will see you in the morning that I knew we were going to spend the night in this remote outpost. The Sergeant told us to keep a few cans of water on the truck, and some rations in case we had to make a quick getaway. After all most of us were Supply and Headquarters Company personal. We were only to be covering for a grunt platoon. They were running late returning back from a patrol to our base camp in Phu-bi earlier that morning. They needed a day or so rest before their next assignment. We were summoned to deliver and protect a section of a forward perimeter that night.

As the sun starting to set low beyond the trees the underbrush around us seemed to illuminate with a red hue. The sergeant and I handed out claymore mines. He said our squad has been assigned the left flank protection for the night. We split up in groups of two and designed a semi-circle that would guard the southern exposure of the big gun positions. One man was to dig a shallow foxhole for cover. The other team member (that was me) went directly out front of their position about 30 or 40 yards to set a claymore mine with a trip wire. We were instructed to settle in for the evening while implementing a 2-hour observation post with alternating shifts.

The underbrush was some 6 to 12 inches high in front of the huge rice patty field beyond another 100 yards. I was very careful counting the steps out to the chosen location. The direction was important so I imprinted in my mind a sight direction from the foxhole to the tree cluster way beyond.

That's it, 40 mid-size steps out, directly at the tallest tree in the thicket on the other side of the rice patty. The six Marines kept an eye on each other as the sun got lower. When we were all comfortable with the positions chosen we began kneeling down to prepare the land mines. All this was being accomplished with no spoken direction. Hand signals and awareness of the task kept everyone's attention. When each Marine finished setting the claymore we stood up and waited until all were complete. The corporal gave a hand signal and we headed back to the assigned positions. When I returned my post buddy had constructed what seemed to be an adequate depression in the earth. At least the hole was just enough to stay below a shadow profile if night flares were needed to direct rifle fire.

Most of my shifts were occupied by combing my eyes over the slightly moon lighted rice Pattie in front of my position. Early in the morning sometime around 3 AM we all heard a Marine frantically call out. Look their coming, their coming, right over there. After about 30 seconds of concentrated fire from at least half the platoon filled the night we heard the order to cease-fire. The flares had that entire section of land bright as the boot camp barracks back at Camp Pendleton. The sergeant spoke out in disgust from behind us. OK men settle down, you've managed to pump about 30 rounds in a water buffalo.

The night was long, and hot with humid off and on rainfall. Bugs were everywhere as our little bottles of repellant started to disappear close to sun up. Each application lasted 5 minutes less that the layer before. The mesquites sounded like mini helicopters hovering for a landing when the bug juice started losing its strength. It was an automatic alarm that brought you out of sleep in seconds. They seemed to know exactly where your ears, mouth, and nose were located. Those dive bombing insects always heading straight for the glory holes on cue like warriors of survival themselves. A blood meal was their reward as it also left a welt the size of a quarter.

Just before sunrise at my deepest sleep moment we were awoke by the firing of the battery of 105's. It was relentless for over an hour of continuous bombardment of the objective. Feeling the concussion of air being sliced, then the sound of the huge chunks of lead being hurled to the hillside beyond always felt powerful. We watched the explosions over 2 miles away dot the hillside in a manner that suggested nothing could live through that concentration. It later was identified to be a softening up operation taking place to go after Charlie and his efforts to build up a fighting force close to their Ho Chi men supply trail.

We held our positions in the early morning hours with rifles pointed out for suspected movement or activity. The counter attack of Viet Cong ground assault was a possibility, but it never came that morning. They could pop up everywhere and anywhere when you least expected it was the reminder from whispers behind the foxhole positions. Mid-morning suggested things were well at hand so the daily requirements of life began to take precedence. After we had a can of C-Rations and fresh water the platoon leader came by our hole and said OK listen up! In 10 minutes go out there and disarm your claymore. We were instructed to secure the land mine for another application later. We will then pack up our gear for the run back to base camp. We leave at midday came the word, or when our replacements arrive.

It was not long before I noticed the foxhole positions and the Marine that went out the evening before to set the mines were standing up waiting for the hand signals. I cleared my M-14, while working the bolt home, and then to the open position a few times. Everything seemed to be in order so I locked and loaded my weapon while pointing the muzzle skyward to signal my readiness until everyone else was set to go.

We started out with the line of sight to the trees beyond. Every few steps I would stop and make sure not to drift off course. At first it was every 5 steps until I got to 30. Then it was every couple of steps looking intensely in front of me with sweeping eyes left to right. When I got to the 36th step with my right foot in the lead I came to an abrupt stop again. My eyes looked intensely at the ground cover in front of me 180 degrees. The wire should be visible by now. The gray/green color of the slightly con caved mine should come into view within at least a few steps or so.

I started to move my left foot forward for the 37th step when a very pro-nounced pressure was felt on my chest. Not like a hand, but like a force with no shape. It was un-settling somewhat, and unexpected at the least. Again I looked around intensely with conviction as my eyes scanned with precise patterns this time. Starting just in front of me and sweeping my eyes about 1 or 2 yards further out each time. The trip wire was still not in view and neither was the claymore mine. After being confident that I was not quite there yet I started to rock my left leg forward again. There it was again, this strange pressure on my chest and mid-section. Once again I rocked my weight back to a balanced feel while beginning the methodical process all over again.

This time my eyes focused directly down at my right leg, not starting out front about 3 feet, but directly down. Silently I heard my inner voice say "there it is". My eyes focused on this tiny, thin metallic wire resting gently within a couple of inches from my right leg jungle boot. A sincere calmness overcame me as I looked up to the blue sky. I had never been an outgoing religious follower. But, at that precise moment the pressure on my chest, and the intuition of aware-ness could not be explained any other way.

Time seemed to stand still for a while. The surroundings around me seemed to brighten with awareness and complete vision. No one in the camp knew what I was experiencing, it was all me. It was my little world right now that could not really ever be explained properly. The feeling that overcame me each time I tried to move forward. There was also the realization that for some reason I was given another day.

This ordeal stayed with me for a few days. Not in the sense of weeks or months during my tour. Only many years later in life did the event start surfacing again. It was because with the dawn of every day in a war zone a new chal-lenge confronts you. A different combat related unexpected task to negotiate. Many of these incidents were filed away in memory waiting for a safer time to surface. When it does return the magnification into PTSD is the ordeals next act. These close calls would replay much later in life when the reality of death was measured in inches and seconds. These combat ordeals would soon become strength to draw from in times of civilian survival also.

Without moving I started looking for the claymore mine again. My eyes focused on the deadly device to my far left and slightly behind me. After dis-arming the mine and packing it away in my fatigue shirt I saw that I was the last one to return to my foxhole. When I looked around everybody was packing up. The night before where we had dropped our gear was about 6 feet behind the foxhole. I asked my post partner about the location of the hole he dug while I set the claymore. Why is the hole so far away from where we staged out gear? He said that after I left with our claymores he had decided to dig in over here because there was less vegetation or obstruction a little farther forward. That statement had clearly explained the reason my step count was off. It also confirmed why the percentage of fatalities and wounded in action by friendly forces became the totals that were just about equal to the numbers actually killed by the enemy.

Simple mistakes that occur even after the solider has been so careful will be the reason for his and other deaths. I think we are all given the equal gifts to perceive what is about to happen. Most go into a situation blinded by thoughts, or visions of other agenda about to happen, or happened in the past. In war one must stay acutely in tuned with the very moment you are in. We must trust the sixth sense, and the feelings our universes places in front of us. When it does happen, we are more apt to pay attention and adjust accordingly. A perfect example of a similar situation occurred just about a year and a half later while working for a Florida police department as a civilian. To this day I believe the only thing that saved me was the intuition or sixth sense again. This ordeal I will explain in another chapter.

We packed up our gear and started the convoy back down the red dirt road. There they were again, those kids on the side of the road begging for food. A few guys in the platoon were starting to throw the kids some food. I got into position and dropped several cases out the back tailgate. We all just set and watched the pack of beggars rip and tear through the food cases as their silhouettes shrank in the past. Some seemed to know exactly where things were located and concentrated on a cretin section of the case. The bodies got smaller as we motored quickly back. Soon they were out of site as we made our way back to headquarters and the security of the huge unit 3rd Bat. 4th Marines position. Replacement troops had rotated in early that morning and were waiting to receive their jungle gear. No rest came for me until the day's activities had been complete again.

DASHBOARD LUCKY

We shipped over with 3rd Bat., 4th Marines on the USS Paul Revere in early 1966 and set up camp in Phu Bi outside of Hue, Vietnam. That summer, I transferred up closer to the DMZ with Headquarters Company 4th Marine Division.

It was a place called Dong Ha. This trip eventually led us even further North outside the village of Cam Lo. It was the last stop before Hell. The Rock Pile even sounded like death, and it was only a few miles further North of base camp. The strategic advantage of owning that hill was the view of the DMZ.

This old dividing line can be viewed on historical maps and at the time it separated the country in two's then called North & South Vietnam. Its geographical advantage came with 750 foot high sheer cliffs, a good view of the river, and a 360 degree look at the terrain below.

North Viet troops from the 324B wanted that location bad, and proved it on several occasions in late 1965. Saving Mutters Ridge and the Rock Pile during many rain storms was a daunting task. The 3rd Battalion 4th Marines managed to hold ground in the Quang Tri region that year. The many battles did require the battalion be taken back to Okinawa and replacement troops brought in to regain strength from past rotating, injured, or KIA personal.

That's where I joined the expedition in late 1965. This rebuild effort was staged at Camp Swaub, Okinawa and took about 2 months to accomplish. The return trip to the same place the Battalion came from in Cam Lo and beyond started with a slow boat ride aboard the USS Paul Revere.

At night we sat on deck anticipating the war we were heading into. Many images of old combat movies, photos, and stories heard growing up in peace time came to mind. We were still doing our day to day exercise routines during that trip so it was an exciting time of anticipation.

No boot camp training film or obstacle course could have prepared us for the beach head landing off the Red China Sea.

Our ground troop platoons had already relieved the Marines that were there for observation and artillery guidance when I arrived at base camp in Cam Lo.

Supplying our squads on the Rock Pile was mainly limited to daily chopper drops. Occasionally, when weather or close incoming resistance dictated, a route by ground was scheduled. I made that trip on two different occasions on a work horse vehicle called a mule. It's a small open top flatbed, low geared piece of equipment. It managed fresh water cans, heavy ammo and rations while negotiating rough paths.

During the early history of operation Prairie, the North Vietnamese Army tried unsuccessfully to re-take the hill on several attempts. The first time I went through the area, I noticed the cost of those fights in the form of an eerie silence surrounding the American military inhabitants.

We were a supply convoy on this trip so the task of getting the goods up that sharp incline fell on us. By the time we accomplished the mission it was starting to get dark. Choppers were not going to lift us or the equipment out of there so we had to spend the night and head back with air support spotters in the morning.

The troops holding the Rock Pile position had been pulling guard every night and were exhausted from lack of sleep. My recent experience in Phi Bi taught me what that was like. I knew when it was your turn to sleep you could not manage more than 10 or 15 minute doze-offs for the next two hours.

The entire campaign of Operation Prairie was a solid effort by Marine General English to establish a presence at the Rock Pile to prepare for the constant threat of Viet regular regiment 324B attempts to retake the mountain. It was a very important time that summer of 1966 between Operations Prairie and Hastings. The artillery support for this sector would come from my duty station base camp at Cam Lo.

Cam Lo was where my supply company opened for business in an ole French concrete building. It was a left over dwelling from the previous French occupation. The roof leaked on rainy days creating red mud, and when it was dry, the dirt floor would generate puffs of annoying dust. Why I was assigned that building was never questioned. It was only about 10' X 16' at best, but was somewhat better than being in a tent.

There was a wall down the center dividing the interior space. The front elevation had two doors. The dividing wall inside had a pass through door with an upper half-door to allow co-mingling to both sides. It also had an 8' high fenced back area about twice the size of the building. Sharp razor wire on top of the fence served as a warning to our POW captives as not to attempt a climb over.

My half of the structure is where we kept all the boots, socks, ammo belts, rifle slings, helmets, rain poncho's, extra fatigues, sundry supplies and whatever they dropped in on us from Da Nang the day before. The other half doubled as an interrogation room for the POW's, or a logistics area where lower grade field officers would plan patrols. Regular meetings with medical, and chopper personnel were a common occurrence. I was always within ear shot of all planning and business that went on under that roof. It gave me insight into what happened on each patrol as well as the upcoming activities of the next day or week.

This was Headquarters, 4th Marines and it seemed to fall to me to be in charge of the supplies for the company. They never really told me this; it just became obvious after some time. Mid-ranking Marines, lower level officers, and anybody that needed something came by and wanted to befriend me. I took the assignment in stride and began taking things one day at a time. When I look back, it becomes difficult to comprehend this all happening to me at the tender age of nineteen. I turned 20 only six weeks prior to rotating back to the states on that tour.

One day a South Vietnamese officer driving a foreign model vehicle similar to a jeep but not a familiar American model, pulled up to the supply hooch. I instantly had a weird feeling about him. His smile was much too big, he was dressed way too sharp and had metals from South Vietnam that I did not recognize. He kept calling me Sargent, but surely he knew the difference between a Lance Corporal and a second level NCO. Then he started trying to give me a pistol. It was a nice looking small piece. It was French made, and I would be the only marine with one like it. I said, "No thanks and asked him what I could help him with today"?

He said he needed some jungle boots and wanted to trade. "Can't do it", I said, "these are for U.S. Marines only". He switched tactics and said, "OK, you buy from me for only 25 piaster." This was approximately 25 dollars in military money. That's about when I started getting too busy to talk anymore so he drove off. Afterwards thinking about the encounter it felt like he just slipped away.

Thinking back later it just seemed to be his routine. He would return every other day or so until he had talked me into taking a drive with him to test fire the pistol. To this day I do not remember why I agreed, but off we drove. It was just the two of us when I saw the comfort and safety of the area melt away to my rear.

This was by far the dumbest thing I did while in Vietnam. Damn we were headed north and all I had was this little pistol. Nobody went down this road without a fully equipped convoy in tow. What kept me on the mission was that I really wanted the side arm for a future extra level of personal protection.

Many times in that combat theater I would think back to my childhood memories for similar circumstances of the moment. If I survived back then, well just maybe I can find the magic to survive this new challenge also. Here is a memory I drew from during the incident while driving to test fire the pistol that day in Vietnam.

If you've never experienced moments that scare you so bad it creates uncontrollable shaking it will be hard to put yourself in my place at the time. These feelings are so profound that one can instantly pull them up from the deepest part of their memory.

It was the summer after our 5th grade and I was high atop Arizona's Canyon Lake road bridge's upper trusses clinging to life with every muscle I had in my body. Being frozen with fear was not what I had imagined would happen when we all jumped into the back of their older brother David's ole 55 Chevy in Phoenix that warm August morning.

We were laughing and excited about the money we had received for diving in the murky gof course lagoons of the valley all summer collecting golf balls. Here I was a few short hours later on the verge of tears with everyone hollering at me to JUMP, JUMP Clemmons, You can do It!

I could not climb back down. The silver painted steel was too steep. And I couldn't jump because it looked like it was at least a mile to the water. The voices below became more distant as fear grew and took over as I stood on those silver trusses.

Time had stopped! I don't know how long I had been up there when I looked over my shoulder and saw my friend David climbing up the truss. He was saying, "I'm coming up there and I'm throwing your little ass off this bridge

Clemmons". Thinking to myself I said, "Well kiddo you've got about 30 seconds to either get brave and jump or get pushed off." Pushed off, hell! If that happened I could get caught up in the steel bracing and tumble to the road hitting everything on the way down.

As if on cue, calm came over me. I stopped shaking and got a smile on my face. All of a sudden I understood how frogs took their leap of faith to the next mossy clump in a lagoon. I knew how a bird must feel just after it lifted off from the branch. Then I imagined how a broad jumper just straightened his legs and flew for 10 feet. Surly 10 feet would be enough to clear everything below. That was the last thought I remember as I let the visions give me the courage to jump.

I took one more look over my shoulder. David was only about 15 feet away when I pushed off. It seemed like at least a 10 minute flight. I had started picking up momentum when it dawned on me that I had not thought about the landing. Common sense or the soon to be cultivated sixth sense must have told me to keep my feet and legs together. My arms were at my side and my eyes were as big as half-dollars. Everyone laughed about that jump all the way back to town.

I proudly added that jump to my "I did it" list. I had earned the right to walk among the bravest. I wore that deed like a badge of courage with an engraving proclaiming, Gary Clemmons jumped off the Canyon Lake Bridge. Most kids wondered why in the world anybody would do that. But in my circles it was a rite of passage. A level of achievement only the few, the proud, the bravest could possibly accomplish.

This same Vietnamese officer came to be known as the resident interrogator of our POW's. The word was that he would brutally intimidate prisoners not yet even classified as the enemy. My days would often be interrupted with sounds of discomfort coming from that room. I knew it was forms of torture and interrogation. The idea of this South Vietnamese officer being a double agent was not yet in my ability to comprehend at this young age.

A prisoner tied up and standing in front of a light bulb for 2 or 3 days prior to an interrogation event was something everyone just assumed I was isolated from through that wall. Many times I would step through the pass thru with extremely mixed emotions. Many of these people could have just been sympathizers for survival only. Yet they were still subject to war crime punishment and mostly for accounting purposes. I do know that continued exposure to war business this close has had lasting effects.

This activity would all take place within a few feet of my side of the building. I knew the Vietnamese officer had a bad side, but he could turn it off like the light bulb he made the prisoners stare at for days. After an interrogation, he would come through the common door asking me for boots and underwear. He would be beaming with confidence and drunk on the power he felt in his role as interrogator. I never gave in to his demands for supplies and called him a clown on many occasions.

I finally said to him about the pistol I'll have to find out if it works properly? The South Vietnamese officer smiled again and told me in broken English with a French accent to come with him in his jeep. "I will drive you out of the camp for target practice". When I broke for the lunch break, he picked me up.

I remember how nervous he appeared. The horror of this little jaunt out of base camp hit home long after we returned. We were a few clicks (miles) from the camp area when I heard a loud bang in my face. It sounded like we had thrown a rod. Hell, I knew what that sounded like because my Uncle Paul and I threw a rod in an old Dodge coup headed out to Lake Roosevelt one hot summer day when I was about 14.

It also startled the ARVN officer into a shaking frenzy, but he just floored the open-cab jeep and stared straight ahead. I would occasionally look down and see his knees quivering un-controllably. He must have been as scared as I had been on that lake bridge 10 years earlier.

We traveled another mile or so before pulling over to the side of the road where some rubbish had been thrown. We were far enough away from the compound so I fired a few rounds. Everything seemed fine. It was a semi-automatic pistol so after shooting a few rounds I said, "OK, lets go". He kept telling me the pistol is still loaded, there is round in the chamber. That's when it was my turn to smile at him. "Yes, I know. Drive back to camp a little faster this time". The pistol was pointed up and to the left past my ear aimed just inches from the front windshield of his jeep the entire trip back to camp.

While he was driving the obvious show of fear was hypnotic as I started getting extremely nervous myself. I scanned the terrain in all directions at lightning eye speed. All the while recalling that day on the Canyon Lake Bridge wondering how I was going to survive this one.

We headed back with that 4 banger going as fast as it could. I was hanging on for dear life. The bouncing ride back ended and I handed him the money for the pistol. Getting out of the vehicle, I noticed for the first time a huge deep, fresh, shiny 1 inch by 3 inch mark on the dashboard in front of my passenger seat. The scar on the metal told me the round must have come in over my shoulder, hit the dash and then taken a ricochet past my left leg and down under the seat on the driver's side.

He turned white as a ghost when I pointed to the scared dashboard.. He just gripped the steering wheel as hard as he could and stared straight ahead for a couple of minutes. We were stunned, confused, and coming to reality of what had happened. I somehow gathered my thoughts and went back to my supply office never taking my eyes off of him until he drove away.

My legs started shaking as I sat there on my office box chair in a state of frozen shock. It took me another half an hour to re-open shop for the afternoon. I promised myself I would never, ever do something as stupid as that again in my life. Thinking about it later in the evening, the incident led me to believe I very well could have been the luckiest Marine in Vietnam that day.

The incident became burned in memory for the rest of my life. The ordeal took on even a more profound meaning when another situation developed about a month later.

The little French concrete fort was next to our Battalion Med Station as mentioned. One might get a good visual by remembering the series MASH. That's what Army calls it, but Marines call it a B Med Station and it had none of the war time amenities or humor shown in the TV series.

The same ARVN officer came sliding to a stop in front of my office door one afternoon with a Marine in the passenger seat. The Marine had been shot in the shoulder and appeared to be unconscious. I rushed outside as several corpsmen and Marines carried him into the medical station.

My eyes never left the Vietnamese officer. He kept saying loudly over and over again, "Sniper! Sniper!" He was pointing to the North. "Just over there, Sniper! Sniper!" A few officers started scrambling to get a patrol put together.

In the excitement, the officer stopped yelling about the sniper and took the opportunity to slip away.

He drove slowly, turning the jeep around in front of me. His driving skills seemed precise and accurate as if in slow motion. He passed by very close to me and our eyes met briefly. This time he did not smile, salute, nod, or afford me the happy little wave. It was just a glance. As the years passed, the incident was burned into my memory. A deep resonating voice would always echo in my ear when I recalled that brief but haunting stare.

"That could have been you Marine". I have mumbled those words many times throughout my life after surviving that combat tour in Vietnam. When recounting his demeanor during that time he always seemed like he was acting. Leading a double life could have been the reason. There are documented historical accounts of a two way South Vietnamese officer discovered in the I Corp sector where I was stationed for most of my tour. I have always felt that had to have been him.

I later made a makeshift shoulder holster. It was my personal secret that no one ever knew about. It became a part of me. It was always there waiting for the dumb ass that might decide to whip my butt. I'd be damned if I were going to make it thru a war just to get home and be taken out by a crazed weirdo hopped up on some physic drug. It took a very long time upon returning from Vietnam to stop strapping that pistol under my shirt every day. It was my little secret, my insurance policy; it was part of my wardrobe. I told nobody, and never got even close to really needing it, except once.

The paranoia soon subsided with the help of Music, Golf and a couple of lucky turns in life during the 1980's. I remember showing it to a co-worker one day and selling it. Not for the money but for the release of an era, and the healing of old memories. Many veterans of the Vietnam War went homeless, helpless, and turned to drinking or drugs to forget the horrors. Many were very successful using the ordeal to strengthen their direction. Many others found excellent understanding woman.

Me, well I had issues that were kept secret for the most part. Some things I could not hide like trust, anger, anxiety, lack of sleep with night sweats and social problems. The VA was not a place one would go to in those days. If you did not have a visual physical wound you should move aside for those that do.

RICHARD BURGESS POW-USMC

Just before we moved up North close to the DMZ in Vietnam a strange turn of events took place that has left me with a lifetime memory and curiosity. My first job in Vietnam was working issuing replacement troops of 3rd Bat. 4th Marines their survival gear and supplies. I befriended another private from Washington State by the name of Richard Burgess. He started coming by just to talk and take some daily grind out of the day I suppose. He was an infantry Marine that had been doing regular patrols searching out the enemy.

The letter I wrote the war department some 40 years after the fact in hopes of someday contacting him might help explain the impact this Marine made on me. Incidentally he is the only Marine I met during my entire deployment whose first and last name I remembered.

Here is the letter I wrote to the war department in hopes they would forward it to him, or give me an address. No response ever came.

February 1, 2006

Dearest Richard,

I not only hope this note finds you, but also so deeply wish it to find you in the best of spirits and health. This letter has been a long time in the making. I will somehow try in my humble way to explain how much you mean to me. How much a part of my life you have been to me through these past 40 years. I have always just assumed that someday you would be in front of me with that all-absorbing smile of affection, allow me to explain.

We were in Phi Bia, Vietnam, 3rd Bat. 4th Marines together. It was close to Feb. 1966 when I arrived via convoy from a South China Sea beachhead, "down the nets landing" off of the USS Paul Revere. I believe we were also together at Camp Swaub, in Okinawa just prior to arriving in country. You went to your infantry squad, and I started the process of organizing the Battalions Supply division. I remember being so exhausted the first night that I just passed out around my gear gazing up at the stars.

The weeks and months that followed were filled with extremely hard work. There were mostly twenty-hour days with nighttime guard duty and hard physical labor in bad weather. All of my close calls and ironic fortunate turn of events could never be considered as heroic as what I've heard you've had to endure during your duties and subsequent capture. They are, non-the less, etched in my memory like petroglyphs.

You walked up to the entrance of my tent one day and said "Clemmons do me a favor". I said "of course"

"Mail this tape-recorder back to my family. There is a message on it to my parents. I have a feeling I will not be returning home."

I said, "Burge don't think like that, but OK, I'll do what you've asked." You explained that your company was moving up North the following morning and you had a premonition. You turned and walked away with your M-14 over your shoulder. I stayed focused on you for some time as like I was in a trance. I seemed to somehow know, as you did, that this encounter would be with me for the rest of my life.

That tape recorder was not under my rack the next afternoon when I went looking for it. The young Marine bunked in the same tent with me seemed to freeze up every time I questioned him about the theft of a tape recorder under my cot. It made me very bitter and that bitterness stayed with me. I started stereotyping black men based on that incident that had fueled an atmosphere of distrust that would stay with me for years to come.

Fast forward to Dong Ha, Cam Lo some time later. As soon as we unloaded I started asking the squad leaders, "Where's Burge?" It did not take long for the word to get back to me about your capture. They all knew from the start that you were captured not killed. There has not been a week, and sometimes daily, that I have not thought about you. How you knew something was going to happen. From that moment on I knew there was something more than just the 'normal' human senses. I used that knowledge and power to survive through my remaining tour and the rest of my life. I never forgot you, Burge. I live for the day I'll be able to reunite with you in person or on the phone. I will not be complete until we have that opportunity. I have only recently been able to talk about our experiences in Vietnam for the first time. I've lived with survival syndrome since then. The VA clinic here sent me to a counselor, who asked me one simple question. What do you remember most about your war experiences? My answer was one word.

Burge!

This letter was sent, but never received by Richard. The military has a very protective routine of keeping former POW's whereabouts a secret. I only found this out by what has to be another of the strangest of circumstances.

About a year after mailing this letter and getting no response, I had come to the conclusion Burge did not make it or, if he had, he was now deceased. Then one day I received a small bill from the VA for medical care earlier in the year. I had already paid the bill and had copies of bank checks to prove it when entering the VA financial office that day.

The lady at the front desk was extremely nice and quickly researched the issue. When she found proof that I was correct she began the credit back process. While she was working on the credit, she began to read my file. She saw my records and realized I was a Vietnam Veteran from 1966. She asked what company I had been with. I must have broken into her train of thought because as she was trying to tell me her husband had been in 3rd Battalion 4th Marines the same year. We spoke the words at the same time. There was a moment of silence as we wondered how ironic that could be. She repeated that her husband was in the same company at the same time in Vietnam.

I listened intently as she began to explain that he had been very active in keeping in contact with men from the outfit. Her last question as we finished up our business that day was "Would you like to talk with him?" I told her I would very much like to talk to him and gave her my number. The last name on the nameplate on the desk was not familiar so assumed her husband and I had never met during our tour in Vietnam.

It was about 7pm that night when my phone rang and her husband and I started to get acquainted. Of course we had the same stories and recalled the same operations. This conversation was interesting, and I thought how strange it was to have a phone conversation in Prescott, AZ under these circumstances so many years later. We began to wind the talk down that evening when he said, "Gary, is there anybody from the company that you would like to get a hold of? "I said no at first but on second thought decided to ask the question.

I said, "Now that you asked, it would be nice to find out what happened to Richard Burgess. He began to speak in a matter of fact voice and told me he knew Richard. He also had his phone number and knew where he lived. I began breathing fast feeling excitement like I hadn't felt in years. We finished the call with him saying he would send Burgess my contact info.

The next day while sitting at my desk I got a phone call from an area code I didn't recognize. I had spaced the idea of receiving a call from Burge and almost ignored it. When Richard began to speak in his deep earthy tone my eyes started tearing up.

We talked for over an hour about his capture, injuries, our lives after the Marine Corp, children, wives, and current health conditions. One question kept nagging at me until I finally found the courage to ask.

"How in the world did you make it day after day in that POW compound for 6 and a half years?"

He began to tell me how he thought of his life in reverse every day. He would wake up thinking about the last thing he remembered before getting shot. That was me Clemmons! Then he would go as far back in time as the day would allow. He sometimes would get to high school, sometimes going back to early childhood memories.

I told him about all the mornings I would wake up and wonder what happened to him after I had returned to civilian life.

Burge and I kept in contact weekly for the next 3 months. I learned of his life as a 100% disability vet. The drugs they prescribed during the early years of his return, the reconstruction of his elbow and shoulder from being shot up then dragged down a tunnel shaft. It was hard for me to picture the 6'2" 200 pound young football player just out of high school as a skeleton of less than 90 lbs. He lost his ability to taste, he had rickets and complications to overcome nobody would want to endure.

Sometime shortly after we had started getting reacquainted he called me early in the morning with his new plan.

"Gary", he said, "I'm changing my life. I've asked my current wife for a divorce and I'm moving with my two kids. "I reassured him that to take charge of his life was absolutely the thing to do. Then he started laughing and said, "Guess where I'm moving" (Silence) "Prescott, Arizona!" Not long after Richard was settling into my hometown. He rented a nice house from another military retiree and enrolled his kids in school. I had mentioned to him on many occasions that

I was still working at my career and would only be available occasionally on weekends. We did not get to spend a lot of time together during the following 12 months. Not near as much as we wanted, that's for sure.

A Marine Corp reunion was scheduled by Jim Gresham here in our hometown. Jim was in the same platoon and had welcomed Burgess home when he arrived back from POW captivity. The reunion was held at a top-notch nostalgic turn of the century beautiful hotel in Prescott, Arizona. Burge and I were booked as the entertainment with me singing 2 or 3 Vietnam songs that I had gathered over the years. Richard was the guest speaker and recalled his experience as a POW, connecting deeply with the Marines in attendance that night.

My family gathered Burge and his two kids up on several occasions for a bar-b-q or various functions. We worked on our trucks together. We would get together and talk about the war and survival. The following year I got booked with a country show in Nevada. Burge would come to see the show and always enjoyed the spotlight and recognition when he was introduced as a POW veteran. He handled everything so gracefully.

He is an American hero. All who came in contact with Richard Burgess became fascinated with his recollections of capture and confinement. He has an easy-to-laugh attitude and a good nature that is still intact. The effects of PTSD and the old battle wounds are there, but the soul is still all American.

All in all being with Burge brought me full circle with my combat tour. No one but Burge and I will ever really understand that day in Vietnam when he told me he had a premonition, a feeling something bad was going to happen.

When Burge walked into the tent that day in Vietnam the encounter became a lifetime changing event. By all accounts story of two combat veterans being reunited could very well been end of story. But there is one more valuable lesson learned from the incident.

After Richard told me he had a bad feeling about the next day's operation into enemy territory, he had handed me that tape recorder. He said, "Gary there is one favor I need you to do for me. If I do not make it back please send this tape recorder to my mom. The address is on the box and there is a recording of my voice. I just wanted to tell them how much I loved my family and the thankfulness for all the wonderful things they had done for me growing up."

The next day's operation and details of the patrol became somewhat of a no response when I asked on several occasions the following week. Half of the rifle company's in the battalion moved further up north so I assumed Richard was with them. Within a day or two I noticed that the tape recorder was not under my cot either. As mentioned earlier in this chapter the Marine that bunked a short distance from me under the same tent seemed to get nervous when I mentioned the missing tape recorder. Well assumptions can be very harmful, so let me explain.

Within a few days of our reunion after all those years, Richard and I were visiting and I tried to tell him how sorry I was that I never sent that tape recorder back to his family in Washington. The subject seemed to be a bit taboo with him. He became distant and unconcerned when I tried to get forgiveness. I continued to bring up the subject of the tape recorder. Burge kept changing the subject and ignoring my need to be forgiven.

A few days' later Richard called and asked if I would be home later on. I told him I would and to come on over. He shows up with the old tape recorder that looked very familiar.

Here, he says, I brought you a gift. You can have the tapes too, because they were erased by the government when they gave me back all my belongings after I got back to the States.

Burge explained that he had stashed many things in his compound tent the day he got captured. Even though it became a conversation piece with my family upon my return I've never had a need to use it. I think it only fitting that you should keep it. I assumed from that point on that he had returned to my tent that same evening in Vietnam. He must have retrieved the tape recorder and took it back to his tent the same day he gave it to me. As I recall the only time I had left my work area was for chow call later that night. He must have felt a confession of sorts was in order once he realized I had carried the burden of losing the tape recorder for all these years.

We both let go of the mistakes that were compounded by both our actions that day. I wish the prejudice I allowed to color my beliefs that day had never happened. Stereotyping is not justified under any circumstances. Even Burge saying he should have left a note when he came back to retrieve the tape recorder should not have been necessary. It was just another war time injustice that happened.

It was all over now and we were alive. His parents and family had dealt with the years he had been a POW and now that was over.

It is rather strange, but I learned a valuable lesson from something that never really happened. I had always felt like I had not secured the item for safe keeping until I could get it mailed. I learned from that mistake and to this day if a task is on the agenda, I get it done immediately. It's an obsessive quirk that gets laughter from time to time. For the most part it has served me well in several professions.

Yes, I received a valuable lesson and Burge's parents were spared hearing his voice and believing they would never see their son again.

Even though he has now settled close to his grown children in a different state I still think of him daily. We will always be connected because of that war and a surreal premonition.

PHI-BI WATER DEPOT

The sweat was pouring off my forehead and down under my armpits like an Epson salt mixture. The giant pink tablets of salt we took every morning were the only relief available from the heat. The slightly fading, spider web-cracked, brown leather seats glistened with perspiration and white salt lines. The open wing windows blasted a heat wave when you drove fast enough, but the door jamb was too hot to rest your arm on.

The sudden realization that I was driving by myself in this defenseless 6X military truck filled with empty 5-gallon water cans jumped into my mind with a bolt. Usually, this re-supply run had at least two of us. An M-14 pointed outside the shotgun window and sometimes an M-60 or 50-caliber machine gun pointed over the top of the cab.

What a hell-hole country this is I thought. It's downright embarrassing to see people live like this. The begging for food, the ugliest language I thought ever muttered from a human being. There were bare feet, rags for clothes, strange food and stench everywhere. At the time, these thoughts were fueled by the lack of any cultural understanding or respect.

I can still hear Mrs. Love, (my childhood friends mother) saying, "OK you boys, time to go take a swim in the canal and get some of that dirt off of you.

Great Idea! We jumped on our bicycles and quickly headed for the 16th street falls in North Phoenix, and we might have a quarter between all 3 of us. The two brothers that lived down the street were a year apart and I was in the middle.

We did everything together during those hot summer months. We played little league games then scooped up golf balls at their dad's driving range. Just diving for golf balls late at night in all the local golf course lagoons was good entertainment.

Sometimes we even built tree forts. OK, we were poor, but we were living clean, had decent cloths to wear and the neighborhoods didn't smell like a sewer. If we got up early enough there was always orange juice, milk, donuts and other good stuff on neighbor's front door steps to pilfer. It was all good until the guilt set in. That's when we doubled back at a later day to do free yard work. Thinking back, I suspect they all knew we were the guilty pack. Somehow things must have been a bit more forgiving back then because we never got in any trouble for having an early breakfast.

Now here I am alone on a rutted-out ole dirt road on the outskirts of Hue city Phu Bi, Viet Nam in 1966. I began to think about my 14th St. buddies as I crept up to the water depot. Where were they now? The ones that took care of me, gave me protection, and seemed always to be in my corner for support. The ones that made sure no harm was to come in a tough situation.

As I've mentioned earlier, back in the hills of Oklahoma I must have acquired what some would call a 6th sense. I think most of us have known that feeling when you just know there is something that just doesn't feel right. It screams at you to beware, don't be curious. Just get the heck out of there and never think about what might have happened later.

Here was that feeling again! I let the Marine Corp 6 X troop carrier truck come to a slow stop in the sweltering heat. I looked up about 200 yards just to my right but I saw no activity under the water tank which wasn't normal. It was a complete ghost town with heat waves rising like a mist from the desert floor of Arizona. Wait, that's back home, you know, where things were predictable and certain. Things like rattle snakes, lizards, jumping cactus, quail or neighborhood dogs running free looking for handouts.

There was nothing, it was just too damn quiet. I focused and refocused over and over. It was just not right. Instinct told me that my stationary time was limited. If something was wrong, it would not take long for my presence to be challenged.

This was odd in every way. But what do I do? The entire 3'rd Battalion, 4th Marines were counting on me to fill these 50, 5-gallon water cans. Those grunts and I needed to rinse the ugly rice patty filth from our bodies daily. That stench from the jungle, rice paddies, body funk from patrols, Agent Orange dust, mosquito repellant and just the crappy air this hellhole reeked of. Surely it's just a gap in the activity. Let me give it some time. I'll just sit here for a minute and see what develops. My mind was slipping back and forth like a time machine in a movie script. I remember pulling my M-14 close and reassuring myself the ammo clip was in place and at the ready.

While sitting there my mind briefly jumped back in time to a theatre balcony. It was the summer of my 7th grade in Globe. Arizona. That's where I met a girl my age that was overly developed. She and her girlfriend, obviously the same age, just plopped down beside me and started talking. Her boobs were so big I couldn't see anything else. The next thing I remember was her guiding my hands towards the open buttons of her dark blouse. The contrast of color made her breasts look even larger than I imagined. She started kissing me with those beautiful red lips that seemed to pucker on their own. What was this, her tongue was pressing my lips apart as if to say "let me in" you fool. It didn't take much persuasion as I felt her sweat mingle with mine as our breathing doubled. She seemed to effortlessly take me thru a routine that was much more common to her than me.

I started thinking how nice it would be if she was here right now and we were in that cool air-conditioned theater to while away the summer instead of this unbearable heat of Vietnam. Normal thoughts for most 19 year olds I would assume. The only difference was that now one could not act on the impulse. A substance called salt peter was added daily to all meals the battalion made. So an occasional thought was all a solider could muster. Any desire was damp-ened by the food additive and rightly so for the job at hand. This routine, or its long term effects just becomes another topic buried in the soldier's history of a combat tour.

The past and present were rocketing back and forth as I sat in this foreign land. I remember thinking that I was perspiring as much now as when I was in that Globe, Arizona theatre balcony only a short 5 years earlier. What was the movie? Have not a clue and never have had since. But now I was sweat-ing from the oppressive, swampy tropical heat and a fear of the unknown just ahead at the water depot belonging to the South Vietnamese.

That thought must have snapped me back around. It was not even a U.S. controlled compound, just one that we came to trust. What's to say those South Vietnamese didn't just run for the hills and not defend their watering hole. With that thought, and a new quick re-evaluation coupled with the 6th sense thing it was time to slip the gearbox, with only a slight grind, into reverse. I backed the big bulky truck with its empty cargo slowly away from the compound. After about a 100 yards in reverse I did a 3-point turn. The maneuver felt natural, like a seasoned stock car racer, and I headed back the way I had come, smoking the clumsy rpm's, back to the battalion campsite.

When the truck came to a stop at 3 / 4 Marines supply headquarters, four or five Marines started gathering around the rear tailgate. Before I could get out of the cab I heard a few cheers when the tailgate was lowered and the men found nothing but empty water cans.

I started walking to the supply tent office telling the guys that had gathered around me that the water depot was closed. When the Sergeant turned to see who had walked in the hooch, our eyes caught.

"The place was abandoned", I said. He then explained, "We heard right after you pulled away that the water compound had been taking on sporadic sniper fire this morning. They radioed and said they would be closed the rest of the day. We had no way to get a hold of you so assumed you would figure it all out sooner or later. The battalion was worried about you out there alone like that. Did you have anything to report?

I just stood there for what seemed like more than a few seconds. My respect for higher-ranking Marines kicked in so I did not repeat what I was thinking. One would think they would send a jeep with a couple of guys to protect a vulnerable water supply truck driver.

Instead my mind raced as I replayed the experience in my mind. It became apparent I had tapped into that sixth sense. I looked up and just said, "I have to get back to work, there are replacement troops due in mid-day so we have to make ready to issue gear. "You'll have to send another driver later when things are confirmed all secure". I turned and walked away thinking as long as I had something to do, he would not order me to do a future run, at least not that day.

For the rest of the day the ordeal played out in my mind about what might have happened if I had driven into that water compound without being acutely aware of my surroundings. This ordeal set me up for the remainder of my combat tour. Those triggers and awareness situations were plentiful going forward during the next 10 months. If I had not paid attention, I'm sure it would have meant I would be returning to Arizona in a body bag like the ones I helped load onto choppers after a jungle operation skirmish.

The replacement troops arrived on schedule and I issued them their last bit of combat necessities. Backpacks that would hold extra dry socks, rain ponchos and individual C ration meals. This assortment of personal items would vary with the needs of each Marine.

I remember the work being extremely hard for the most part. Working with your shirt off a lot to stay cool produced a tan I had never gotten even from the hot, desert sun in Arizona. Constant processing and lifting heavy boxes of personal supplies and rations for the troops was a daily routine. The physical demands that started a couple months earlier in Okinawa produced many finely muscled and defined bodies. I bulked up to 167 pounds on my 5'8" frame with a slim 30" waist.

After returning to the United States, I was stationed back at Camp Pendleton, and I was in the best shape I'd ever been in my life. Many of the NCO's in my company told me on several occasions I should ask for a transfer to the physical fitness division and help others keep fit and healthy. I did not think too much of these compliments or comments because the transfer just sounded like a lot of work to me.

One day, out of the clear blue and completely by surprise, my Staff Sargent handed me transfer orders. It was devastating to say the least. There was no choice but to accept it. The numerous warnings for being late for roll call after weekend liberty had finally caught up with me. My weekends in Phoenix had come to an abrupt halt. I sat there under a shade tree reading every type written line over and over.

I was being transferred to Marine Barracks, Charleston S.C., a Naval Submarine Base. Wow, I thought, that's all the way on the other side of the United States. I started asking around about what Marines do on a Navy base. Sure enough, I was being transferred to the MP's. It was the duty of the Military Police to guard ships both in port and when they were out on sea deployment. Marines were also responsible for base security.

After arriving and getting a short training course, I became a guard at the base's Main Gate. Good duty by most standards, for sure. I was checking ID's, issuing temporary passes and working rotating shift assignments. Like any duty station in the Marine Corps, a sense of excellence was expected in all your actions. This was a high profile military establishment and surely a very important strategic location.

Main gate guards had to be dressed top notch, groomed and snappy. That lasted for a while but the temptation of liberty kept luring me on a nightly basis. In a few short months, it also started to show. A couple of night before party slips later; I got transferred to Quantico, Va.

Quantico was base headquarters for the FBI, CIA and Officers Candidate School and was located just outside Washington D.C. It was a great duty station and very nice part of the country to be in. I did not take advantage of all the historic sites the area had to offer. Of course I gained a much stronger appreciation of our country's history later in life.

A sharp looking Marine introduced himself when I arrived at my assigned bunk and cubical. We got to know each other after a short time. His demeanor, interaction and communication skills were excellent. He soon told me who he was and then things started making sense. My new roommate was the current Mr. Marine Corps.

He had not been exposed to the war like I had and with just a few questions it became apparent his military experience had been very sheltered.

We soon headed to the gym and it was apparent he felt right at home in that environment. He asked me to spot him and said he would do the same for me. It soon became obvious that I was only about half as strong even though my physique made me look in better shape.

Officers and FBI or CIA students alike would drift over to our workout area exchanging greetings and they would ask if he would be their personal coach. I soon realized this was going to be his job. It would also be mine since it looked like we were going to be a team. I lasted a few weeks but it soon became quite obvious I did not like the 5 mile runs before breakfast, daily workouts, and the new strict, healthy diet changes at all.

This young man was part of the Marine Corps' new PR campaign. I'm not sure where I was to fit in but I never really felt comfortable. I soon found myself cutting gym time for the enlisted men's club in the afternoons playing music in a few different band projects.

A advertised exit strategy appeared when President Nixon enacted what they called Project Transition. It was for military personnel with 6 months or less remaining on their enlistment who were not planning to stay in the service. The veteran would also receive training to help him meld easily back into civilian life with a profession he liked. It was a noble gesture. After signing up for this new program, they placed me in, of all things, an inventory office job. I was not there much because my new 5-day week Radio and Television school training was in downtown D.C.

I found out that the perfect class for me was starting at the exact time and that I was eligible. The National Academy of Broadcasting was based in Washington. The idea of being a disc jockey, sitting in front of a microphone at a turntable playing music all day was extremely attractive. My entire childhood had been comprised of music.

Because of my early home life, music was in my soul and here was an opportunity to further my career in music and make my life bearable after four years in the Marines.

I drifted away from my new friend, Mr. Marine Corp, in 1969 and moved to off base housing. My duties in the Marine Corps had become limited to a few hours per week and reporting my attendance records at the Broadcasting school. I excelled to the point of having a radio show in Warrington, Va. even before graduating from the class and getting my honorable discharge from the Marines. Producing revenue-generating commercials, programming and sales seemed to come natural.

If I look back at this time period, I realize the early signs of PTSD were even then beginning to change my personality and way of thinking. I could not go fast enough, wanting to live life to the fullest. Sleep became something I did for a few hours a night. I had full-time jobs, even a part-time job and finished out my enlistment with the dream of returning to my hometown a hero. A combat survivor could surly get some breaks in his home town.

"COMBAT, LIFE, & THE SIXTH SENSE"

What could possibly be the reason for assuming one's life has been entertaining or interesting enough to write a book asking such profound questions? Who am I, Who have I become, what have I contributed to this world that is meaningful and can someone please help me make some sense of it all?

Other than finding that twin everybody is supposed to have, all of us are similar in some way or another. If categories were established, mine would be under "only child, no father figure in household and on your own at a young age". That title seems rather generic and many people would fall under the heading. It's what happens along the way that surely makes us who we are. As one might file away individual journeys and experiences, the percentage of common traits keeps getting smaller. Hopefully, it's then, we all begin to feel that uniqueness, that understanding that we are each individuals unlike any other.

As I sit here at 'command central' in my 3rd bedroom/office space, a large window frames the day's activities, serving life up in real time. I swivel around and look at bookshelves I have packed with material. I've stashed these books over the years with the idea that someday I'll read them all. I felt reading them would make me so much wiser, a better person and more informed. Since I've officially retired at least 3 times now, I can start enjoying social security, small VA disability checks and a modest retirement account and, yes, start reading all those books.

Looking at the shelves, there are only a few topics I have collected. It seems my interests are about Music, Construction, and a little History with emphasis on the Vietnam War. There are also some self-help books and a few books speculating on the possibility of ancient alien space travel.

The section of books on music includes guidance and instruction and the business side of the industry. They have been very helpful in my second career as a musician.

As I look over the titles, I realize most of the books include information I can or have used in order to be in control of my life; to be in charge or die, lead or be led into retreat or failure over which I have no control.

Knowledge of wars effects on the combat veteran throughout history has been discussed in books of every generation. There is no better truth than the participants' individual rational of their experiences. The youth of every era pays the price for politicians and investors who feel the need to invade a foreign land. One of the single most accelerants of the war commitment is portraying the foe as humane vermin. A common denominator to spark the conflict is delivering the yarns about the difference in religion. They want to kill Christians, They hate Catholics, or they want to dominate all mankind.

While in Vietnam a solider has access to a chaplain, priest, or clergyman of their religion if requested and if at all feasible. I had that opportunity deep in the jungle close to I corps up by the DMZ that separated North and South Vietnam. My only question to the chaplain before shipping out on an operation went something like this. Now why do we need to kill these people over here? The answer was "God wants us to kill these bastards". Now that was a strong statement to a 19 year ole with very little structured religion history.

So consequently when the war was over, and we appeared to not have won the battle God must not have been on the Americans side. The subsequent lack of any religious involvement after the Vietnam War with many veterans became the norm.

If you are retired or about to enter into retirement, you might not be surprised to find yourself looking back wondering the same thing as many others when finally given the time to think about it. You question how in the world you managed a career and handled the everyday things necessary to maintain a productive life. Especially if you have experienced combat in Vietnam and memories of the war are constantly lurking in the equation? How were all the decisions regarding career, marriage and health made? And how were you able to deal with how the war had changed you; the control issues, difficulty communicating your feelings, trust issues, the change from calm to obsessive caution?

If you are just embarking on building a life after combat experience, do not be complacent. Don't think PTSD is something that happens to the other guy, not you. My symptoms, even though I didn't recognize them, were dominant in the early days. A combination of some luck, experiments to release stress and a passion for music saved my ass.

This book is by no means a "tell all" recap of my life since combat, but I do feel it's important to touch on the topic of drugs.

I went through high school never being exposed to pot, speed or drugs of any kind. Some six years after my tour ended, I was on the road with a real good band. As we traveled from town to town, our back-seat conversations covered a wide range of topics.

Even though I had become used to the lack of sleep, night sweats, memories of close calls in combat and keeping the depression in check, I was still secretly fighting the effects of post war illness on a daily basis. After watching the other band members dip a moist finger in a baggie of orange powdered Kool-Aid for a week, I decided to go ahead and try it out. They talked about enhanced awareness and flashing colors darting in from an array of light sources. Hell, I was already dealing with the same thing without taking any drugs. But I was still intrigued and curios for the main objective at the time of, just fitting in.

My first experience with LSD was intense enough to make me thankful; I had already set up and finished a sound check for work at the club that night. Then suddenly, in a moment of clarity, I remembered the band had the evening off. When we all got to the gig the following night, I realized that neither one of us had slept in a couple days. I don't really remember much about that night which is probably a good thing.

As if obtaining some sort of divine intervention during that almost 3 day high, I became totally convinced I had learned a great deal more about the world and my place in it. The effects of that 1972 summer music tour and the exposure to drugs lasted a very long time. The project ended after a year, but not the silent lessons learned. None of the other players in that band had served in Vietnam or combat. They never mentioned it, and I knew if I were to survive this next segment of life it would be best to NEVER bring it up in conversation.

Youth and the lack of education come into play here. During the Vietnam War if you were in collage you were not expected to serve. Many enlisted personal, and later draftees thought they were buying a scholarship to the collage of their choice after each battle. In reality most veterans filtered back with more pressing priorities like catching up with their demographic. The United States had home loans and collage perks in place upon the Veterans return but it took persistent efforts to capitalize. It was in Veterans rights, not necessarily a combat veteran's right. The combat veterans had an entirely different set of agenda that needed attention before they could move on successfully.....Healing.

I recognized this early upon my return and did seek help in the form of counseling. It was not available to the veteran reaching out. In fact it was discouraged and looked down upon for needing help. Hell man, you're alive what more do you want was one answer I got.

The constant flow of adrenaline in a combat zone is obvious. The concentration and awareness it takes playing music on a daily basis isn't putting your life on the line but it can also be really intense. Now, add in the occasional use of recreational drugs and a person's thought process can become extreme. Being a disc jockey with a fast paced radio station requires focus and some serious organizational skills. I thrived on this daily activity and continually put myself in highly demanding situations. At the time, it was substance for the soul.

Recently on the news, it has been revealed that PTSD therapy now includes experimenting with drugs in small doses. Did I have a significant stroke of luck come my way back in 1971 that helped ease PTSD symptoms? One never knows when something they do might become a life changing experience down the road. I am in no way promoting or endorsing the use of drugs without professional observation and a physician's guidance. Having lived in a time when nobody talked about drugs or about being in Vietnam, I find it interesting that the medical profession is now saying symptoms of PTSD respond to drug therapy.

When I turned 60, it felt like it was time to give something back. I began looking into Non-profit organizations where my time and skills would be useful. There are organizations out there that will take advantage of a person's willingness to help, expecting them to give more than they are willing or able to give. But those are easy to recognize. Being a volunteer for a cause you believe in can bring a great sense of accomplishment.

I asked myself the question, Is that enough? My first venture into volunteer work was with the National Day of the Cowboy. It seemed like a good cause. One day a year was set aside to celebrate the long time profession of the Cowboy. Why not? Cowboys helped shape this country into what it is today.

The Cowboy has a sport dedicated to keeping the importance of the life-style alive. Rodeo is exciting as well as fun to be involved with. But it did not take me long to realize that the glamour of being on a board of directors or holding a chairmanship is only a title and fell short of one's expectations. It might take several attempts with various 501c non-profits because there are some that have self-serving agendas. Finding what is right for you, if you choose to take this route, will take some serious analyzing to make sure you are where you want to be.

My wife and I were in the little town of Wickenburg, Arizona to attend its annual parade and Rodeo. My stepdaughter was going to be riding and car-rying the "National Day of the Cowboy" flag. We had some time before the Rodeo parade was scheduled to start and decided to visit the town's "Little Red School House". The building was preserved for the town through grants along with people interested in their local history. The old school house is where my wife's mother went to school many years prior. I found a yearbook with the name Dora listed. Even thought it was "not her mother", but it non-the less caught our attention. Both of us imagined ourselves back in that time period and we started asking questions of the custodian.

It was obvious to see the building was being used for music. The museum manager explained that retired professional musicians give free traditional instrument music lessons to kids with a desire and the ability to play. Learning to play and perform using the fiddle, banjo, piano, guitar, and other instruments struck me as a real good cause. Later chapters will reveal why this was right for me as well as my wife, Tina.

I listened intently as the lady told us that if they could make use of the basement many more children could be given lessons. She explained that the spiral staircase did not pass the current commercial codes and that they were looking for a contractor to tackle the upgrade. They had the money for the project as there was a grant being offered by a local family. She smiled and turned to walk away and I think we were both a little surprised when I spoke up. But the words rolled off my lips without any hesitation.

I took the renovation plans through the entire process of city council; plan approval, structural and architectural committees. When it was completed, it became one of the most satisfying accomplishments of my life. I believe that volunteering time to similar projects could deliver some peaceful night's sleep for the brave at heart.

"I'll do it", I said. Wow, did I really say that? After her initial surprise, she said I could have the old staircase if I took it out and replaced it with a modern, wide switchback style to the lower level.

The 24 multi-family construction projects I've built to date as site Superintendent will all stand for many years to come. They are most definitely tangible evidence of a career I'm proud of. All I have accomplished playing music also is a special source of pride, as well. But the staircase upgrade has always given me a special feeling of accomplishment. The Little Red School House 501c board of directors presented a plaque of appreciation to the Clemmons family during the official dedication some 18 months after the "I'll do it".

Another achievement that has given me many hours of competition and pleasure is Golf. It has always been a special passion for me as well as most of my close friends. It is a sport that relies on you alone. The "Only You" factor is something I've become used to over the years so golf was a perfect game for me. One has to dig deep physically and mentally to control all the muscles the golf swing requires. Overcoming all the things that can go wrong in the swing, facing down the obstacles; the sport is just downright challenging.

At 64, I survived a four round tournament and won the club's Net Champion title at my hometown Golf Course. It was 4 rounds of Golf grind at its best. The first two rounds were (of) stroke play and the next two eighteen holes were elimination match play rounds. A 12 handicap at the time did not seem enough for me to even have a chance. After the first 2 rounds I was tied for 4th place and barely sneaked into a playoff. My first match play opponent was a much better golfer.

The mental toughness to never give up during times of sure defeat was continuously at the forefront of my mind during the round. I prevailed on the 18th green with a par winning the match 1-up. The next round was for the championship. All week I was thinking about how fantastic it was that I would be playing in the championship round. Even 2nd place would be great. But the day of the final match, as we stood on the first tee box, I had an entirely different mindset.

After all the many things I had accomplished in my life, I now get the chance to win a golf championship. Never give up! I will win. On the first tee, I see that he is an 8 handicap. This means that on the average day he is a four shot better player than me. How will I ever be able to overcome this challenge? At one point, I was down 2 with 6 to go. I had a long talk with myself as I walked up to the number 13-tee box. I willed in a 25-foot putt on the next green, and then fired at another pin tucked behind a bunker on the next hole.

Soon it was time to cut the corner of a dogleg par 4 and I eventually pulled even on the 17th tee box. Not only was I surprised, but my opponent was a little shaken when I said, "That's how it's supposed to be, a good close match. We are all tied up and regardless of the outcome; you've given me a great match."

Having done well to this point gave me confidence on the tee. I focused and drove the ball right down the middle. I rolled in a putt from off the green to pull ahead 1 up. Even though my ball did not go as far, and having a few years on my opponent, I pulled it off. I prevailed on the 18th green to take home the trophy and title of Club Champion. It was a huge accomplishment for me. A determined mindset along with mental toughness must be what it takes to accomplish these kinds of milestones. Winner of the 2011 Men's Club Net Championship will be on the Country Club wall long after I'm gone. Not a great contribution to society, but none the less a very rewarding accomplish ment for me personally.

I have been fortunate in that many men and woman who have overcome difficult backgrounds to achieve their success have crossed my path. I learned early on to never make excuses. And blaming defeat or failure on life's circum- stances just never occurred to me. In fact, failure was never an option. The level of success was the focus. The higher I set my goals and met them, the more likely I was to achieve the respect of my peers.

My accomplishments in Music, the Marine Corps, Construction, Golf and life itself, have far surpassed my expectations and early dreams. What I have done has not necessarily been easy for me for one reason. I have never been able to narrow my focus to the point it would take to become a master at any one thing in particular.

I believe the good times I had throughout my variety of travels became silent propellants in my quest to live a full life. The degree of someone else's perception of my achievements does not concern me. Even though this took many years to understand, it has helped me find peace within. I will not let the opinions of others have anything to do with this hard-earned peace. The satisfaction in our soul does not have to be a public forum. It can be something that keeps us striving for the next opportunity to succeed.

While trying to make some sense of it all I've become mindful of thinking back to what I'm most proud of. What have I done that makes me feel accomplished? Who have I become? All of us may have similar thoughts, but what are mine? Along the road, a PTSD counselor told me it might be best to just start writing about my feelings. He was right; I did find much comfort in getting my memories on paper. Revisiting the memories has produced a profound insight into those things which have shaped my personality.

This book is filled with recollections of my combat experiences in Vietnam and the 4 years I served in my beloved Marine Corps. I hope it sheds light on one thing I believe we all have. "The Sixth Sense"! Some people may possess this gift to a greater degree than others.

I believe at birth we all have this natural power. It appears this gift will be recognized and become stronger as we age or its existence will be denied. I, for one, recognized the sixth sense and began not only trying to develop it but began counting on it. I recognized early on that I could depend on it to help keep me safe and out of trouble. Of course the moment you forget it exists, or pay no attention, there is no evidence of support.

Returning to the West Coast of the United States from combat remains a vivid memory. Military flights returning from the war zone taxied to a designated airstrip hanger. I checked out with the officer in charge and headed for the airport shuttle that would take me to the main Los Angeles terminal. I was really looking forward to the short trip home to mom and my hometown of Phoenix, Arizona.

There were 3 Marine officers on the shuttle with me. They were already dressed in civilian clothing. We shared the usual small talk and then a concerned older officer seemed to feel the need to ask if I had any regular non-military clothing in my bags. Since I had just returned from the far reaches of fighting in the most Northern sector of South Vietnam, I did not. He reminded me that if I wore my uniform in public, I might find myself in some uncomfortable situations.

The officer said I should not take it personally. His advice to me was to just keep my composure, get home and then ease back into society as gracefully as possible. Naturally, I thanked him that day for the advice not knowing what was in store for me. The two men sitting in the backseat listened and gave a nod of thanks, showing their gratitude for the bit of wisdom the senior officer shared with us.

The wait at the airport in Los Angeles was short but also memorable. Some of the people waiting at the gate for the trip to Phoenix and cites beyond were college kids on their way home for Christmas vacation. There were also business folks headed for places east.

I noticed right away that everyone was avoiding eye contact with me. A young student was sitting on the floor over in a corner with a couple bags and a beat up guitar with no case. I was a musician, too, so I decided to stroll over to the guy for some in-common company.

After a self-introduction, I sat on the floor next to him. My first timid statement to this stranger was, "That's a unique guitar what kind of music do you play?" An uncomfortable silence assured that my attempt to be friendly was not going to work. His reply was abrupt but softly spoken. "I would rather be left alone at this time if you don't mind". OK, thanks for putting my ass on the line for you for the past year, I thought. Since I hadn't perfected that reply yet, I didn't say anything, but I sure thought about it.

The chilliness of that concrete floor raced through my body as I sat there trying to come up with an exit line. My future personality would probably have prompted me to say something like "Most good musicians carry their instruments in a case for protection, so is this really like a prop or what"? Instead, I gathered up my things and moved to a space that would minimize any chance of more civilian rejection. After all, I was headed for a happy time. In just a few hours I would be able to give my mom a big hug.

Within a half an hour, the statement made by that senior Marine officer became a (harsh) reality. I realized I should have taken his advice and changed out of my uniform because by the looks I was getting, I knew something was very wrong. The weeks to come would paint a vivid picture of how the American people really felt about the war and its veteran.

The plane started its descent into Phoenix and Sky Harbor airport was a welcome site. It was just before Christmas 1966, and one of those beautiful days that the southwest is known for during this time of year. The short cab ride to Mom's Secretarial Pool office only took a few moments. When I exited the cab, the driver wasn't all that friendly as he barked out what I owed him. He was not about to offer a free ride to a veteran.

I entered the building and left my bags right inside the office's front door. I watched my Mother reaching for her hanky when she saw me walking towards her. The other 8 or 10 workers did not even look up. I hadn't really known what to expect from people at that point but I knew I was getting a cold reception. Mom and I hugged and cried for a few seconds before she said let's go home. She said the boss had said she could have the afternoon off if my arrival was on schedule. I glanced in the direction Mom motioned only to see even the boss was not interested in acknowledging my presence. A thank you was not in order from either side, I suppose.

When we got home, Mom made my favorites; Iced Tea and a Grilled Cheese sandwich. After sharing and recapping the news of the past year, I asked her the question that had been concerning me. I wanted to know why everybody kept looking down at their typewriters avoiding interaction with both of us when we left her office.

Mom took a deep breath and explained that the War was not a popular topic of conversation among the general public and some of the secretaries had boys in High School who could be subject to the draft. She said the people did not support the war in Vietnam and many of them took their frustrations out on the soldiers. A short discussion on this topic suggested that I finish my enlistment obligation and get back home to start a life that was not so confusing.

Before I left for my next duty station, mom made it a point to remind me that being bitter about public opinion for the remainder of my enlistment would only harm my well-being. The days and months that followed, I completely withdrew from civilian life. No matter what anyone thought or did, I was still proud to be a Marine. I was still grateful to be alive and to have survived in spite of it all.

I had another 2 1/2 years to finish in the Marine Corps. Mom made me promise not to volunteer to go back to the combat zone. I profoundly assured her I would not. The rest of my time in the service was spent being a hard working

Marine. From that point on, during leave or off time, I still had great pride in serving but I tried to never wear the uniform in public.

Accepting the fact that we, the Vietnam veterans, were the scapegoats for any angry nation was a pivotal moment for me. This was the foundation I based my actions on going forward. Although being very proud to have served, the bitterness of public opinion and subsequent treatment of the troops upon their return during the Vietnam campaign was demoralizing. It took forever for me to regain the courage to even ask for a date. When I finally did get up the nerve, it came with a brutal reality check.

I had just invited a girl, who was sitting shotgun in my nice 1960 Chevrolet 2-door Impala, to go to a party. There was a long pause, which left the question just hanging in the air for a devastating few seconds. Then she answered with explicit instructions. "OK", she said, I'll go to the party with you under one condition. You do NOT mention the war or your military duty".

She was right because even with my short hair and disciplined military personality, by keeping my mouth shut about the war kept a low dark cloud from descending on the party. I managed to hide that part of my life for a while but over the next couple of years, rage and discontent was building up inside and it wasn't going to take much to breech the weakly constructed dam and create the emotional equivalent of a 100 year flood.

Mom and I had talked a lot when I was on leave. We talked about the challenges with breast cancer she had faced since my deployment. We highlighted some of my more heart tugging letters from the jungle. We laughed about all the good times we had while I was growing up.

Mom knew I wanted to walk through the old neighborhood that evening for old time's sake but before I left she told me there was something we needed to talk about. "I know for the past year you have been sending most of your paycheck money home for safekeeping", she said. Just my military pay alone wouldn't have been a large sum. They only paid soldiers $120 per month at the time and that was with combat pay. But while in country I had become a very lucky and skillful poker player. Since the money was military issue script, it always felt like monopoly money to most of the guys. Many treated it like play money and they didn't think of it in terms of regular U.S. currency as I did. Every time I saved $40 to $60 dollars extra, I would go buy a money order and mail it home.

As time went on, that turned out to be a frequent occurrence because we played a lot of poker in the far reaches of the jungle.

Mom continued talking and then she finally dropped the bomb. My savings was gone. "It's gone, son. Most of the money you sent home is gone." She told me she had missed so much work due to her breast cancer operations, the money had gone for expenses. I felt her pain that evening. Knowing the anguish she had endured because of the cancer was a whole lot more painful to me than not having that money waiting for me when I returned.

I remember holding her and saying it was all right. I told her I would be able to buy a car in due time. Being home and safe to help her was all the reward I needed. I loved my mom. She was all I ever had and I needed her more now than ever before. I was not going to be thinking right for quite some time and I needed her wisdom" It had always calmed my anxiety when I was young.

I was all by myself that early evening in December, 1966. I had left the house and was about a mile from my old grade school and stomping grounds. I took off in a brisk walk. I just wanted to see the school grounds and remember the neighborhood I longed for during my tour. I wanted to take in the smell, sights and sounds and feel the comforts of home that I remembered.

I walked alone as dusk overtook the day. The coolness of the desert air was all around me. I thought of the nights I'd spent in foxholes and how peaceful the nights would be from now on. The acute awareness and adrenaline high caused by the constant battle to survive had dissipated. No more would I need to carry my rifle, grenades, a knife, ammo and the life sustaining tools of a combat solider. I didn't know, as I walked the streets I'd known so well before the war, that soon, I would feel naked and alone without my trusty pistol hidden under my shirt at all times.

Walking through the familiar neighborhoods remembering old girlfriends helped the time fly by. But school ground memories and friends were not enough now. Life would never be the same again. Not after war, not after having to hunt and take another man's life in order to survive.

There were no defragging classes then explaining why the adrenaline continued pumping through our bodies. Or why our subconscious kept trying to rekindle that acute awareness. We didn't know how to stop the need for that high so we looked for it, often creating chaos in public. We didn't know it but we were begging for the attention, someone to see and understand what was pushing us and someone to translate our actions into a plea for help.

It wasn't long before I rounded the school administration buildings and headed for the corner gas station that gave away a free Cadillac every year. Fate intervened that evening as I got close to the familiar station. I saw an old black & white, 2 door 55 Chevy with the hood up. It was the car my friends drove when we had gone diving for golf balls as kids. Even though it was only 8 or 9 years earlier, it seemed like a lifetime ago. I remembered being woken up before the sun came up, heading for the golf course and feeling around the muddy bottom of the lakes until we had found a bucket full of golf balls. As I looked at that car, the relief of being able to share companionship in any form at this critical time in my life felt like nothing but good luck.

I walked up to the car and there, under the hood fixing the Chevy's transmission linkage, was John Love, one of my best friends when I was growing up. I said "Hey there", he yelled my last name and it wasn't long before we jumped in the familiar car and began cruising around our hometown.

For the next 3 weeks there were no rules. Riding around in that hand-me-down car of his older brothers was like old times. We had both made it back alive from jungle warfare in a foreign land. John's combat experience was one of the most dangerous. He carried a radio and would be perched in observation posts that were always vulnerable. We did not know then, that there was much more to overcome. Survivor Syndrome had not yet been acknowledged in our understanding of PTSD. There was Agent Orange exposure that would be directly related to COPD. And the need for control caused a survive-or-die mentality. That mentality would be the first hurdle.

My discharge from the Marine Corp in 1969 began a period of suicidal actions. My first wife had met an active military man just after my discharge and had asked for, and was granted a quick divorce. The war was still raging in South Vietnam with the largest buildup of our troops to date. Updates were on television every night. I could not watch because it made me sick to my stomach. Many of these guys were going to go through the same lack of understanding and transition challenges that I was experiencing. There were going to be more failed marriages and a hostile reception just like I had received in their future.

There was news footage the public refused to admit was happening. I made it a point to never talk about the war. I looked in the mirror every morning, standing there with shoulder length hair; I told myself that it could not have been me over there. If it was me, no one would ever know because I was so disconnected. At least, that's what I told myself daily as I relived vivid combat memories on a regular basis.

The media and our government were not telling the public about the suicide rate of combat veterans. The only time a former Marine of the Vietnam War was mentioned on TV, it was in a negative light. The media also relished in uncovering false claims by criminals who had been caught portraying combat veterans.

I just wanted to forget about all of it so scoring girlfriends and enjoying the party life became my main focus. Many times I would drive 80 miles an hour over the streets of Phoenix plowing right through stop lights and stop signs. The majority of my passengers would be hanging on and screaming for dear life. Most of my friends quit riding with me during that period. Some expressed emotional exhaustion after riding even short distances with me. I would call them chicken shit and cowards and laugh. It took years for me to realize that they valued life much more than I did at that time. The close calls in my civilian life after combat are as haunting as the ones in a combat zone fighting the enemy. The healing continues to this day sorting out the effects our military had creating exposure to activities against combatants and civilians caught in the middle of a war of no consequence.

As time went by, my personal ambition to succeed attracted people to me but my suicidal or verbal comments about their lazy incompetence would drive them away. The years were clicking by and I was not getting any better. Rage was a common occurrence that seemed to surface with the slightest of provocations.

The Military had no Outreach Programs in place. In the 1960's, PTSD and Agent Orange exposure did not exist as far as the government was concerned. As I mentioned before, our government did not report on the effects of combat or the high suicide rate among returning military. I don't think my second wife even knew I had served in Vietnam, let alone a combat zone. Multiple personality traits just seemed to be a way of life for me. I dealt the best way I could. Don't get me wrong, I was able to stay on the fringes of normal society and managed to stay out of any big trouble. But there were some close calls during those times.

It was not until 35 years later that I first stepped into a VA hospital. There were many uncomfortable sessions with my doctors between then and now. A few of my acquaintances with similar backgrounds kept urging me to be persistent, encouraging me to hang in there and assuring me that it would get better.

A lot has been learned by our government and military since that war. They have admitted to facts that have allowed the medical profession to understand and treat many problems facing our returning combat veterans. I see many good things happening with our combat vets in the 21'st century. For those current veterans who are wondering how things will ever be right again, give it some time, get help, and don't give up.

Band Leader / Bass guitar for successful Phoenix, Arizona country band "Stumpwater-Jak"

Early 80's Band Leader for Hall of Fame artist Johnny Western in Paige, Arizona on the lake.

Formed a band with musicians Paul Spradlin & Tony Cook at Reata Pass in Scottsdale, Az.

Ron Keel and I performing in the Country Music Tribute show at Whiskey Pete's in Nevada.

Band Smoke N Guns performing for the 2007 Az. Music Hall of Fame induction ceremony

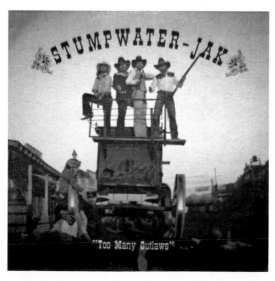

Stumpwater-Jak's Album and self-titled hit record "Too Many Outlaws" 1980

Las Vegas with Ron Keel, Kevin Curry, and Craig Small, "Sin City Southern" band 2011

Popular road gig in Flagstaff, Arizona with Marty Mitchel, Michael Hounshell, & Randy Wright

With Johnny Western back stage after he was informed of his Az. Music Hall of Fame Induction

Marty Mitchel and I digging deep at a Dodge Theatre show in downtown Phoenix, Arizona. 2007

Promo photo in 1994 with the "Ronnie Lee Band", Cave Creek, Az. Song "My Horse is a Harley"

Photo taken by Renee Keel at the Las Vegas Saloon in the downtown Experience area

Getting ready for a dinner show in Sedona, Arizona with "Rumor Has It" in 2005

Pool party's at the Point South in Phoenix, Arizona summer of 2009

Before a Ranchers wedding in Wickenburg, Arizona with Smoke N Guns, 2008

Promo pic by Renee Keel at the Pioneer Saloon south of Las Vegas. w/ "Sin City Southern Band"

Playing a solo segment in a production with Country Music Superstars

Promo shot with Stumpwater-Jak in 1980, Cave Creek, Az

High school days group with Step-Father and friend George Mac Johnson

Stage shot during the early 80's

Combat veterans bothered by the horrors of war and their memories may need to file a Stressor Letter with the VA that contains verifiable research information. Here is the one we filed recalling incidents that haunt the mind. They are short condensed versions of chapters mentioned throughout this memoir. Yours will be unique and specific to your tour, and your memories.

VA FORM 21-0781

Statement in support of claim for service connected

Post-Traumatic Stress Disorder (PTSD)

Gary L. Clemmons

11/5/46

3rd Bat. 4th Mar.

C.O.   J.W. Woodland

March to June 1966

During Operations

Golden Fleece 11, Virginia, Cherokee, Wayne, & Athens

Incident # 1

Down the Nets

W/ 3rd Bat. 4th Marines

We came down the nets from the troop carrier ship The "Paul Revere". It was difficult weather on the Red China Sea on March 20th 1966. I was loaded down with my gear, rifle, and parts of an M-60 Machine Gun. The seas were choppy so one had to time his 'let go' of the ropes to get in the Mic Boat; a lower-the-front-ramp hit the beach boat." I was being stepped on and kicked on from soldiers above as I screamed to explain, "Stand By we have to time it" It did not work, I fell at least 25 feet with all that weight. Of course, landing on top of other troops must have been extremely painful for them, as well. Although we did not receive resistance in enemy fire, the landing did claim 8 Marines lives that day as I remember. The weather and choppy seas became a major challenge. This falling incident is not something one forgets easily.

Incident # 2
Chopper Landing

W/ 3rd. Bat. 4th Mar.

After about 9 or 10 days on ship, we had not received any exercise, sunlight, or mail. After the beachhead landing, we convoyed through the country towards Hue/Phu Bai for the rest of the day. Our company was given sections of ground to pitch camp. The men in my company were all sitting on the ground on the outskirts of Hue that evening trying to collect our personal gear at dusk. That is when the mail call started to boost moral a little. It had turned pitch black by the time my mail got to me.

Just about that time the sound of 2 or 3 choppers coming in for a landing broke the silence. It was deafening not to mention the tremendous amount of wind they generate. There was no lighting in the compound and no lights on any of their birds. We were grasping at everything within reach. When I looked up, the rudders of the helicopter were literally inches away from my head. He finally focused enough to realize he was landing directly in the middle of over 200 Marines. The pilot hit full throttle to recover. That sent mail and gear flying for 50 yards in all directions. When the noise and confusion subsided, I began helping everyone. We were on our hands and knees without light of any kind looking for mail. We soon huddled together and for the rest of the evening we whispered the names written on the envelopes until all the mail was 'delivered'. Eventually I found my gear and made a big pile to fall asleep on. My last thought was this was my first day in Vietnam.

Some 15 years later at a friend's house for a chess game and never recanting that story to anyone before he said, "Here is a book you should read". I picked it up and saw it was a Vietnam helicopter pilot's story of his tour in Vietnam. I thumbed through it quickly and stopped somewhere in the middle of the book. In disbelief, I read his recollection of an incident where he almost landed on top of a Marine one night while trying to deliver rations to a company of incoming troops outside of Hue in March of 1966. The probability of me turning to the page with that exact story was too unbelievable. I slammed the book shut. The incident once again reaffirmed my decision to not talk about the war. Who would have believed me if I had told them I was that Marine and had just accidenlly turned to that page. I have since lost touch with the owner of the book. But for many years now I wish I had written down that author's name.

Incident # 3
Trip Wire Close Call

W/ 3rd. Bat. 4th Mar.

While stationed outside of Hue/Phu Bai with my division, it was routine to deliver rations, ammo and water to the companies many different operations listed above. While accomplishing that task on one occasion it became apparent we would not get back to the company command post before dark. They made the decision to have us stay overnight. Four of us dug 2 foxholes after taking direction from a Staff Sgt. We were instructed to set up one claymore mine in front of our sector for protection and warning. Flares went off over the rice patties we were guarding every 30 minutes all night long. Not much sleep or shut eye going on that night. In the early morning hours, the 105 howitzers starting firing support for the operation's patrols.

We began to retrieve our claymores a sector at a time that morning. While doing so, I felt a presence come over me. I froze! Almost smiling, I wondered what this feeling was about. I started to move forward again but the same strange resistance came over me.

My eyes then began working their way closer to my legs. That's when I saw the faint vision of a trip wire on my back pant leg. My right foot had stepped over it, but the left would have dragged across and released the firing pin of the Claymore only a few feet away from me. I summoned help and escaped probable severe injury, if not death, that day. It was the sixth sense that saved me again. Something I would pay close attention to in combat.

Incident # 4

Equipment & Gear Handout

at Supply Tents &Water Truck Detail

W/ 3rd Bat. 4th Mar.

In most cases, it was 115-degree weather or pouring down rain. Duty was mostly 14-hour days of hard labor under extremely stressful conditions and on occasion even pulling night guard duty. My basic job description was in Supply distributing gear, clothing and supplies to the replacement troops. Over a period of a few months' worth of operations we had a lot of activity. I would ask 10 or 12 fresh new men to kneel down in 2 rows while I handed out everything from mess utensils to backpacks, boots, to bedrolls. Sometimes this gear came back to me freshly washed, but with a lot of shrapnel holes. Some new guys would start tearing up; others could hardly hold back their emotions. I would sometimes go over, kneel down and softly tell them the truth. "Look, we are only experiencing about 5 % fatalities with another 10% wounded. Look at it this way; there is an 85% chance you are going to make it just fine."

Here I am, 19 years old, a supply man, trying to console men while I had no psychological training.

I also had the duty of loading up a 6X truck with about 50 empty five gallon water cans daily and driving them into the city limits of Hue to re-fill. We were short on men one day so I was asked to "just go by yourself today, it would be fine." When I was about 200 yards from the tower and water well, I noticed things seemed a little quiet and abandoned. It was usually frantically busy with plenty of ARVN milling about to guard the compound. I backed the truck out of there returning 3 or 4 miles back to my company command post. I told the supply sergeant it was temporarily closed and that he should check into assigning a detail to search out another water depot.

We heard later that evening that the water supply station had been taking on sporadic sniper action that morning. By this time, I was totally trusting in my 6th sense. To this day, I believe it is what saved my life then and many times after.

Sometime just before operation Prairie I had written a letter to my mother back home in Phoenix, Az. I was completely exhausted so the not-so-encouraging letter sent mom into a panic. She called a stateside Chaplin who dispatched two very concerned men to my company in Vietnam. They talked to me for a couple of hours. It was only a few days later that I was transferred to 4th Mar. Headquarters. My new assignment was even further north, somewhere close to Dong Ha/Cam Lo and just a short distance from the DMZ. I do not believe they did me any favors. We were as far North as any division ever made camp for the wars duration. This act of sending me deeper into the fire taught me to never trust the people your confiding in. It could be the Law, the newspaper, the mail or investment counselors. Never trust anyone with your feelings and rely on your sixth sense at all times.

Incident # 5
P.O.W Compound

W/ 4th Mar. Hdq. Co.

June to Dec. 1966

In support of operations

Prairie, Florida, Dodge, Jay, Pawnee 1, and Hastings

One morning I was transferred up North to 4th Mar. Hdqs Co. in between Dong Ha & Cam Lo. There was an old French building with 2 rooms. An area behind the building had been made into a P.O.W. compound for the captured VC. The room next to my supply office had a half door to the front and a pass through door to the prisoner interrogation room. Many times that room would ring out with violent dialogue in Vietnamese. The routine would be to make the captured stand under the light bulb looking directly at it with his hands tied behind him for 2 days or so being slugged, hit, slapped and other punishment. If he closed his eyes or buckled down on his knees, the higher-ranking ARVN solider would show up and put a pistol to his head or in his mouth. At times, he might cock the pistol and push the weapon into various parts of the prisoner's body. They usually broke down by day 3 and told the guards everything they knew. They were then thrown behind the building in the fenced compound where the only shelter from the elements was a crude built doghouse. I still remember those moans and sobbing from the young men out back. Being in the next room while this type of interrogation took place time after time are memories etched deep that will never be erased.

Incident #6

Dashboard Lucky

W/ 4th Mar. Hdq. Co

June to December 1966

The same Vietnamese interrogator would occasionally come over to my office and speak broken English trying to befriend me. He would always ask me for boots and underwear. One day, he brought me a pistol that looked really nice. It would be perfect to have under fatigues. He wanted 25 dollars for it. I spoke up, "How do I know it works properly?" He said, "Come with me in my jeep. I will drive you out of the camp for target practice." When I broke for the lunch hour he picked me up and off we went. I remember how nervous he appeared but did not put facts together until we returned. We were just a few clicks from camp when an ear-splitting bang went off in my face. It sounded like we had thrown a rod. It also startled the ARVN officer but he just floored the open cab jeep and stared straight ahead.

We headed back with that jeep going as fast as it could. I was hanging on for dear life. Getting out of the vehicle, I noticed a huge, deep mark on the dashboard in front of my passenger seat. The scar on the metal revealed an angle that suggested the round came in over my shoulder then ricocheted down under the seat on the driver's side. He turned white and just gripped the steering wheel for a few moments. I was stunned and went back to my supply office and reopened shop for the afternoon. Later in the evening when I was reliving the incident, I decided I very well could have been the luckiest Marine in the country that Day.

Incident # 7
B-Med. Station

W/ 4th Mar. Hdqs. Co

June thru. Dec. 1966

The next tent over from the French-made concrete fort that housed my supply office was the B-Med Station. Over the next 7 months, that field hospital played host to some of the most gruesome and unpleasant sights of wounded who needed quick lifesaving procedures. The casualties during operation times were heavy, the atmosphere extremely stressful. I ventured in to the big tent that looked just about like the MASH episodes I watched years later but without the horrifying screams of agony that, at times, could not be silenced. I would sometimes be summoned to the chopper zone a couple hundred yards away to help unload the body bags or severely wounded. Delivering them to the tent was absolutely horrifying. If one used their wildest imagination, they still wouldn't be able to describe the sights and sounds.

M-60 Mine Sweep Detail

Incident # 8

W/ 4th Mar. Hdqs. Co

June / Dec. 1966

I was chosen to join other Marines and manually sweep a suspected mine field area about a half mile from the command post area near Dong Ha. We were traveling in the back of a 6 X troop truck. It came to a stop and the Lieutenant started explaining what the objective was. This very large Marine sitting across from me had turned out to be a stone-cold drunk. He would sleep walk in our tent at night and piss on every ones rack and belongings. We complained to the Sergeant many times but to no avail.

What this solider did that day was very scary. He was a company ordinance clerk, supposed to be highly trained in weapons. While sitting directly across from me, he stood up and grabbed at the loaded bolt-action M-60 machine gun. He started out aiming it down but more and more rotating towards me. I started scooting over and finally jumped up screaming "What are you doing?" Don't point towards me."

Everyone was watching and concerned while I scrambled away. He let the bolt action of this M-60 machine gun go to the closed position and it slipped from his grip with a metallic thud. This all took place in a matter of a split second. An M-60 has a fixed firing pin. So the round went in the chamber and fired all in one swift motion. The mark on the bed of the truck was proof it would have taken me out quickly. I was screaming at the top of my lungs. Everyone saw he was so drunk he could hardly focus. The detail jumped off the truck and started milling around in complete silence. The Lieutenant was so shaken by the incident that he ordered everyone back on the truck. The weapon was taken away from the soldier and we returned directly back to the company compound. We never saw this Marine again and I never asked what happened. I've always hoped they would have re-assigned him stateside and hopefully to a detox ward for his own survival and well-being.

Incident # 9

Richard Burgess

W/ 4th Mar. Hdqs. Co.

June thru. Dec. 1966

(See Letter to Richard Burgess)

Incident # 10

C-130 Escape to Freedom

W/ 4th Mar. Hdqs. Co.

December 11th 1966

The time was nearing for my rotation date. I had painfully counted each day for months. Three days prior to my departure date the company clerk came to my hooch and asked if I would mind giving my seat to a Sgt. who wanted to get home in time for his wife's birthday. I did not really want to do it but he promised I would rotate the following week, no questions asked. With more persuading, I reluctantly gave in.

Departure day had arrived, I made it and I was alive. We loaded in the C-130, some having tears of joy anticipating the long ride back to the United States. We all strapped in the cargo nets as the pilot taxied out to the starting point. The runway at Cam Lo was made up of metal sheets all connected together and each slab full of holes. Full throttle, we headed down the runway only to feel the opposite thrust a few seconds later. The pilot explained we were a little overloaded and he needed to try it again.

This time we inched our way to the very end of the runway. Off we went again with all the Marines lifting there feet and grunting to help the twin-engine bird to lift off. Again, the pilot shut it down. He turned it around and headed back to the starting point again. This time he came on the loud speaker and said, "Well men we are going to give it one more try. If it doesn't work this time we are going to ask 10 Marines to get off and catch tomorrow's flight to Saigon".

The C-130 lunged forward with a moan and shudder. Someone started shouting go, go, go, go, go. It didn't take long before everyone was shouting in unison, "Go, Go, Go!" This time he did not shut it down. When I could no longer hear or feel the metal track beneath my feet, I knew we were off the ground. One of the crewmembers came back to the cargo area where we were all cheering. He began to speak as our noise settled down and said, "If you guys only knew how close that one was".

COP OR DISC JOCKEY

It was a different type of climate in the small town of Del Ray Beach on the Eastern coast of Florida between Miami Beach and Fort Lauderdale. We had traveled there to take my wife's sister home. She had come to stay with us during the birth of my only son. The weather was not that different from Vietnam. Humidity and heat came together between sunrise and dusk during the extended summer months. There were basically two seasons in Vietnam. Hot and dry or hot and wet. Here in Florida, it was hot and humid during summer months but winter brought some relief in the form of a blanket of moist, chilling air from the ocean.

The drive from Marine Barracks, Quantico Va. was supposed to start with a one week visit with my wife's family before heading on to Arizona. The adventure of starting a new life after the military had been anticipated with excitement for over a year. As it turned out, one week turned out to be an 8-month trial employment period at the police department in this small Florida coastal town.

A year before my enlistment term was over; President Nixon had enacted a plan called Project Transition. My four-year military stint with no disciplinary actions allowed me to take full advantage of the plan to achieve a life-long dream. The qualifications simply stated that if a veteran wanted to return to civilian life after combat service, he could go to school full time during the last 6 months of his active service. If I signed up for the plan, I was also required to keep up with our military obligations. Those would usually consist of pulling weekend duty and some evening assignments. Other stipulations were that I stay in a top physical condition ready to return to war, keep my barracks inspections current and tear gas readiness preparations and rifle range qualifying up to date.

As a young child in grade school and high school, I would sneak a transistor radio either under the covers or at a low volume in my bedroom. The disk jockeys talking between records were all so upbeat and funny. They were likable and popular. They seemed to be part of the pulse of what was happening in every community. I wanted to be just like them, so when this chance presented itself, I took full advantage.

A small ad in the base newspaper glamorized a school in Washington D.C. only 50 or so miles away from Quantico. The National Academy of Broadcasting seemed like a place that knew exactly what they were doing. Besides, how could any radio station in America turn down the chance to hire one of its graduates?

I was sure I could handle full-time school and my military responsibilities. It also gave us the opportunity to have our child born in one of the finest military hospitals without any expense if the child arrived before my discharge date of May 31'st, 1969 . Kenneth was born at Walter Reed Medical Center downtown Washington D.C. on May 20th. 1969.

I dug right in and worked an accelerated curriculum with gusto. The course covered everything from T.V. reporters, copywriters, announcers, advertising specialists, speech and the technical knowledge of keeping the equipment up and running. The class also prepared us in securing an FCC, 3'rd class radio-operating license. In those days it was a requirement to have this license even if all you did was spin records and give the news. The course covered just enough to teach the proper protocol and on air etiquette. The standard procedures of keeping a signal frequency adjusted to the correct call sign and keeping records of all emergency-broadcasting requirements were also mandatory during that era.

Less than halfway through the course, I was offered a part-time evening shift at an FM radio station. It was not too far from our nation's capital. It was called an easy listening music station with the call letters WEER. The station's library was filled with big band giants, iconic instrumentalist and Symphonic renditions of the latest pop and rock tunes. In those days, a disc jockey could reflect his personality or mood by the choice of material he played. Flipping the switch to the open position with 10,000 watts behind you was nerve racking at first but it became second nature after a few weeks. The station manager would call in occasionally giving me suggestions. We reported the temperature and the weather every third of fourth song in a soothing voice and finding new variation became a routine.

I learned a lot about radio station operations during time at WEER. A big reason I was able to take in so much was the amount of time allowed between segments. I kept my mind occupied and boredom at bay by snooping around learning the station's setup and reading everything I could get my hands on.

One of the last classes at broadcasting school was the fine art of selling advertising and producing jingles. In order to get a passing grade, we had to pick a business and produce a jingle for final evaluation. Well, I took it a few steps further. One day our instructor had business elsewhere and had trusted the ten or twelve students to continue the board shift rotation while completing the daily assignments. That day I decided to check out the attic above the broadcast booth of this 14th Street building in downtown Washington, D.C.

In the dusty space above the drop ceiling, I found boxes of old commercials by the Andrew Sisters and other popular bands and groups from the Big Band era. They were called doughnut spots or continuation theme aids for local business needs. I came across an old 78 record for a generic car commercial ad that had voice breaks in the singing for new sales information on a 60 second and a 30 second timed ad. All I would have to do is insert business, brand, location and other local information into the non-singing segments. It was perfect for creating a familiar and friendly theme for a car dealer's account. It seemed apparent to me that these stashed jewels had not seen the light of day for at least 25 years. At one time in this building a working radio station was intact, not just a broadcasting school.

My assignment had just gotten a lot easier. On my way home that evening, I drove by the local Dodge dealership and wrote down the address, phone number and any particulars I could use for production later. The next day I took my turn in the production booth and knocked out a fantastic package with sweet singing voices alternating with my dialogue hype for my neighborhood Dodge dealer. It sounded so professional that it even shocked me. I was proud but a little embarrassed later when the instructor used it as an example in front of the class. These particular doughnut spots had not aired in sometime, so they sounded fresh, and not familiar to everyone's ears.

As I approached the Dodge dealership on my way home from school that Friday evening, a thought came over me. Why not pitch these two spots to the management and just see where it goes from there. It was so exciting to know I had produced these spots and I did not want to see them end on a shelf with only a passing grade to show for it.

You know how they say timing is everything? As in music, survival, sales, investments etc.

I had decided not to be nervous about the presentation because there was absolutely nothing to lose if these jingles were not sold. My discharge from active duty was in just 5 days and counting, including the weekend and I wanted to hear the fruits of my labor on the air before my family and I pulled out of town. If it did not sell, oh well, I had a demo tape of my voice for future job interviews.

This kind of confidence can mean all the difference in whether a sale is or is not made. I had spoken to 2 men when I entered the building and told them why I was there. One went to the reception desk and I heard the P.A. click on and a voice telling the manager there was someone to see him. The 2 salesmen then took me to an office and we all sat down. While I was waiting for the dealership manager to enter the office, I cued up the small portable tape recorder. At the ready, I sat back and began looking at one of their sales brochures. When the manager entered the room, I was surprised to see he was only a few years older than me. He had piercing, deep blue eyes, blond hair, was neatly dressed, and looked very distinguished. He was what a person would expect a dealership manager to look like. It appeared to me the lower level management team had run first interference with this cold call radio ad salesman. But now I was talking to higher management. It heightened my confidence level even more.

I purposely did not go right to the meat of the sales pitch. The other two gentlemen in the office sat quietly back as we discussed the Marine Corp, tours of duty, families and the usual chit chat. After they all had been curiously eyeing the tape machine humming on the desk for some time, I sprang into action.

"Sir, I've made a couple speculation commercials for you. Since I live in this town as well, I feel a need to encourage you to add some quality radio jingles to your sales arsenal". "Continuing to use military terms to present the pitch flowed with ease. When the boogie swing girls started singing about his dealership his eyes remained fixed on the reel-to-reel tape. At precisely the right moment, I reached over and flicked the lever to the off position. I had decided to say nothing at this point, because up until now, he had been the one reserved in communication. That's where a fidgety 20 seconds of silence took over.

When the manager did speak, he asked one simple question.... How Much? I learned then and there, how important timing was in the negotiation process. My mind quickly, calculating a fair price; so what should I charge? As if a seasoned salesman had taken over control, I blurted out, "Twenty-five will take care of everything."

Now in 1969, 25 bucks went a long way. Heck that was two full tanks of gas that could get me half way across the United States. The manager looked at the rosy-cheeked older man. A slight head movement must have been the authorization telling him to go cut me a check. The time it took to take care of that, we talked further about which radio station he would like to have as executor over this master jingle tape. I suggested the station most of the Marines listened to. It was located just outside of town near the front gate of Quantico, Va. where FBI agents and Marine officers were trained. He agreed and I assured him I would deliver the master tape to the radio station no later than Monday morning. I told him he should deal with his normal account manager about buying a running 90 day schedule for saturation coverage.

Walking out of that dealership, I was thinking what a great start this was to my new career. I still believe this event was the both of us needing each other at the precise time for success.

I sat down in my 1958 Chevy Impala, and looked down at my first jingle production check. It was made out to me for $2,500.00 dollars. I remember starting to shake and tremble a little as I pulled out of the parking space and drove down through the rows of cars parked on the dealership's lot. I kept praying I wouldn't get confused trying to find my way out of this maze and have to drive back by the sales office. Is this a dream or have I just pulled off a heist of the year. I concentrated on avoiding eye contact with any other employees on the way out. I was sure any second someone would waive me down, point to the office and tell me they had made a huge mistake when they cut the check. But nothing happened and I was smiling as I drove my eleven-year-old Chevy back to the base where I was scheduled for evening duties after chow.

That Chevy's straight six-banger engine ran good on thick black oil. It had needed a starter for the past six months but I always parked on a slight hill and it didn't need to be moving very fast for me to pop the clutch and fire it up. It was a miracle it ran and hard to believe this car, won in a poker game at Camp Pendleton, had been so reliable. Now, I thought, I could trade her in on a new model. But I would have to stay on base tonight as I had a meeting scheduled with my military career counselor bright and early the next morning.

The following morning I reported to the commanding officer's building. Looking sharp but feeling surly, I admitted I was curious as to the meaning of this meeting. The Lieutenant assigned to meet with me at this morning's discussion was the same officer who had promoted me to Sergeant three months earlier. He had received information about my graduation from Radio school so the re-enlistment bonus had jumped from $1,800.00 to $3,500.00 in just those few short months.

This was a tremendous amount of money in those days, especially for a non-commissioned officer with only a high school background. He said I could have the choice of almost any duty station I asked for. He even said, Mr. Clemmons, you'll probably get promoted to Staff Sergeant within a couple years".

We stared into each other's eyes for a long 10 seconds or so. After what happened at the dealership the day before, considering this offer was out of the question for me. I was thinking about a career in radio. It was indeed a lot of money the military was offering this 21 year old. I knew I might have to be stationed far away without my wife and son who was less than two weeks old at the time. I knew Kenneth's mother had dreamed about this opportunity all her life. Being a military wife and having the security of a check made out to her every month and the base commissary was the pinnacle of success girls from the poor side of Charleston, South Carolina dreamed of from the time they started middle school.

But after having so many close calls, I was sick of the war. I had seen way too much death and destruction to even chance another tour. I told the Lieutenant it appeared to me the war was escalating and ground troops were going to need more radio operators. I told him I knew the kill ratio for radio operators was very high, and I also knew he couldn't assure me I would not have to return to the war zone. I finally found the nerve to tell him the offer was tempting, but no thanks.

He had done his duty as a counselor except for making what sounded like a rehearsed statement. He said he wanted to remind me that I could retire from the Marine Corp with a monthly pension at the age of 38. Then he asked me again if I was sure I wanted out. I told him yes, I positively wanted out. I will never forget his final statement before filling out the final discharge he said,

"Thirty eight will come quickly and you will remember this conversation. He was right, I've never forgotten.

My wife, son and I drove to the East coast of Florida that next Wednesday with only a couple misfortunes. A local cop gave us a ticket that had to be paid on the spot so I wouldn't have to go to jail for driving without lights at dusk. We also had a new born baby in the back seat belting out blood curdling screams over everything and nothing.

For a short distance that day, we were travelling right behind a drunken couple who was weaving all over the road. We saw the driver lose control and crash into a tree. We pulled over to help and saw that the lady was banged up but was going to make it. The driver was slumped over and the lifeless expression on his face was all too familiar to me. We stuck around for a while finally leaving when we heard the ambulance's siren in the distance.

Within a few short weeks after arriving in Del Ray Beach, Florida, I received an offer to apply at the local City Police Department for a radio dispatcher position. Unknown to me at the time, police departments all over the United States were recruiting former Marines. I did not want to live anywhere except Phoenix, Arizona, but after much persuasion, I filled out the paperwork.

It was a slam-dunk interview with a captain that looked mysteriously like the cop standing next to Oswald when he got shot by Ruby. I was called into work the very next week. Training was not necessary as I would be behind a microphone all the time and not out in a patrol car. It became very intense but interesting work. It was actually similar to a combat zone as there were about 10 squad cars, 4 detectives, 4 motorcycle patrolmen and a Sergeant on duty every shift.

After witnessing a few episodes of traffic traps and strange ethnic-related incarcerations, I started to get the feeling that the town was a little corrupt. The jail was only steps away from the main office radio room and booking area. It reminded me of the little French fort in Dong Ha, Vietnam with the POW compound right out my supply hooch door. The prisoners would scream out their innocence from time to time. I fell into a routine of passing out about a half pack of cigarettes almost every shift. It was like an insurance policy. If there was a break out, they might not come after me on their way out.

I was always in a major saving mode putting away all the money I could for the future. It was never enough to just have a job. I always had to have a second job, too. Many times I also held a 3rd part time job even though it seemed somewhat excessive even back then. This is definitely at least one of the reasons I plowed through 3 wives in the years to follow.

My first part time job in Florida while working at the police department was at a golf course in the next little town over called Boca Raton. Watering the greens in the evenings and staying clear of the live gators in the lagoons close by was entertaining but could get a bit tense at feeding time, for sure.

This job only lasted a couple of months. An officer at the station told me about an out-of-department patrol shift coming up. It sounded easy. It was a midnight to 4 am shift. He told me I should have time to get home, rest and have breakfast before I started work again at 8am. It sounded good to me and dragging a hose around at the golf course for 4 hours every day was not a lot of fun. Plus, the unmarked patrol car pay was better.

A private firm was hired by the state to patrol interstate highway 441 just a few miles in land from the coastal main road. It was a North/South route that went all the way into Miami. The patrol took about an hour each way, so a couple trips down and back was the shift duty. They furnished a new vehicle, gas card and key to the pump at the shift station.

I had been on this patrol for a few weeks when the quiet hum of the big block Ford I was driving was interrupted when a question I hadn't thought to ask popped into my head. What am I supposed to be looking for? All I remember them saying was for me to be on the alert for suspicious activity.

There was no siren or lights on the car, so pulling over speeders was certainly not the objective. I rarely ever saw another vehicle on the two-lane road during my shift. Most of my time was spent dialing in radio signals with the best reception absorbing techniques used by different disc jockeys.

The paycheck was always there at the station on Tuesdays like clockwork but I was starting to feel unproductive writing the same thing on the security sheets every night. "Nothing out of the ordinary to report at this time!"

I had just finished the far Northern turn around one morning when I remembered a class in the Marine Corps that had taught us about different ways to keep a post secured. The instructor told us setting a pattern, then interrupting that pattern by doubling back to see if potential threats had figured out when they could safely carry out subversive actions.

I decided to put it to the test. I did my normal turn around very slowly at the intersection before heading south towards Miami again. Everything appeared to be normal. There was no activity, or autos parked in the area. The lone structure, a building that looked like an old vegetable barn, sat on one corner. It was open on 3 sides with a wall in the back. There were always packing boxes stacked up everywhere making it look like it was used as an occasional weekend fruit or produce stand. There was a large field of tomatoes or some type of crop behind it. I had never really bothered to identify what was being grown there .

Kicking that big engine with the huge four-barrel carburetor up to cruising speed was an unmistakably distinct sound. I rolled along for about a half mile before gearing the automatic transmission down one level at a time. I purposely did not use the breaks. When the big luxury Ford slowed down enough, I did a turn around without using the breaks and was quite proud of the maneuver. Turning the lights off and radio down, I slowly began to creep back toward the intersection.

Sure enough, when I had made it about halfway back, I could see the silhouette of a vehicle cross the road and head for the barn structure. The older pickup truck did not have any lights on either. The driver slowly headed towards the barn, creeping along under the dimness of a small wattage area light. My dark, unmarked patrol car kept moving towards the barn at a crawl. I would slip it in and out of gear just enough to keep moving.

At a distance of about a hundred yards from the structure, I knew I would be partially blocked by vegetation. I slipped the car into park. The only thing that broke the silence in my vehicle for the next few minutes was the sloshing of gas in the tank after the abrupt halt. I sat there intensely observing activity in the area for quite a while.

There were three men silhouetted in the moonlight methodically unloading their truck. The vehicle looked like a farm truck that would be used to haul hay. The only difference was the removable, open-air side panels. One guy was on top throwing down what looked like bales of hay while the other two carried them into the back part of the barn.

I had managed to sneak up on the location so covertly that the men continued working unaware I was so close....... at least, they hadn't seen me yet! My mind was racing as I tried to analyze the situation. Now the question was why would they be working so early in the morning? Was it too hot to do any work in the daytime? Why did they have their lights off? What were they unloading?

It was 1969 and I was under the impression that most drug deals took place in big cities like San Francisco, Los Angeles and Chicago. Mostly cities that had universities where draft-dodging students sat around on big park benches looking confused and taking refuge in puffing pipes while dancing to Deep Purple, Cream or occasional sitar music. Movies portrayed deals going down in dark hotel rooms above Jazz lounges where the smell of pot filled the air. Refer Madness scared me, but that seemed a bit exaggerated even back then.

I spent my last couple of years in high school before the Marine Corp in a remote area of Oklahoma. That is where doing an illegal substance meant getting caught with a jug of moonshine grandpa gave you for doing a chore the day before. Besides trying to smoke some dried up banana peelings while stationed at Marine Barracks, Charleston, S.C., I had no idea about the complexity or vast business the drug trade had become.

I had just returned to civilian life after four-years in the Marine Corp and I was still trying to catch up on how much things had changed while I was in the service. But, as I sat there, some things were beginning to make sense. The massive drug culture which had sprung up across the nation offered huge payoffs to suppliers. The area I was patrolling was only 90 miles from the coast of Cuba and was obviously a drug drop location. Marijuana was coming off boats and was being distributed inland for destinations across America.

Holly molly! I'm sitting right here in the middle of a drug delivery. I had no sooner had the thought when I noticed all three of them had frozen in place and were staring at me sitting in my car only a short distance away. It was a stare down for at least 2 or 3 minutes. No one moved a muscle.

Thoughts were bombarding my brain. What should I do now? To be a vigilant patrolman, I should ease up there and ask what was going on. Every time I started to reach for the gearshift, a force or pressure came over me. It was the same pressure against my body that I had experienced in the minefield just a couple years earlier in Vietnam. The men had not moved since the moment they saw me. One was in the back of the truck on his knees looking directly at me. The other two froze in mid-stride. I remember thinking that I could die here this morning. This situation was not something one single guard patrol officer should be required to handle. My mind raced back to the training instructions the gentleman gave me at hire date. The words "observe and report" finally surfaced. My muscles relaxed and I was able to put the gearshift into reverse and slowly backed out of there.

When I turned in the keys that morning, I asked the shift dispatcher to make a log entry saying that I'm giving my notice to the part time patrol job. I also told her I would not be taking the patrol car out from that day on. I continued working with the police department for a while but a few months after my experience with the drug dealers, the job became intolerable. Besides, I had decided it was time to return to my desert home in Phoenix where a wide-open and exciting career in radio was awaiting.

When we arrived in Phoenix and I immediately began looking for a radio job. A few things came my way but soon wife number 1 told me she wanted to move back to her home of Charleston, S.C. I had moved my mom in with us so I could take care of her and she was not well enough to make such a long move. It hurt to put mom into a nursing home to accommodate the wife's request, but I did. Only a few short weeks later we were as far as Oklahoma City and were staying there while visiting my step-parents. I had the most powerful luck of all time when Buck and Teddie Mattox took me in after moms cancer treatment enabled her to take care of me.

We got up one morning; she looked at me and said, "I Want a Divorce."

I was on the road back to Arizona within 3 or 4 hours. She and my son stayed with my step-parents and she started dating the young military man she had danced with at one of my shows the prior weekend. Buck was a good singer and had helped to propel my music in high school.

She called about a month or so later to let tell me her fling was over and she was considering coming back to me. I laughed and told her not to bother because I had moved on emotionally and did not want to have anything to do with her. I told her I would take my son and raise him if she would let me. She abruptly hung up and she must have called the boyfriend right back because they were married just a few weeks after she had called me. There were a few phone calls from her and a military lawyer called me weekly trying to persuade me to allow the new husband to start adoption proceedings for my son. They said the boy would have better benefits and perks through military aid than the courts would give him through me. She remained with her new husband for many years after his active duty discharge. He was an aviation mechanic and seemed to be doing well in the Washington State and Las Vegas areas.

I moved on with my life which included recovering from the loss of my wife, son and mother within a 24 hour period. I had stopped in Dallas to call Phoenix and let them know I would be returning within a couple days. My aunt Dorthy told me on the phone that my mother had passed away just hours prior.

Here I was in my hometown and completely alone. Most of my childhood friends were still deployed or had moved away. After four years in the Marine Corps and a horrific tour of combat exposure in Vietnam, I had to provide for myself with no family, no friends and no support system.

It eventually started coming together after landed a job as the morning disc-jockey at KMND, a powerful AM & FM signal in Mesa, Arizona. Playing drums 6 nights a week at a Scottsdale night club called the Scotch Mist for a couple years helped me get through the nerve-racking and confusing time when I was trying to transition into my new civilian lifestyle. It seemed the need for both music and radio took over my life. KAFF, a respected station in Northern Arizona put me on during a five night a week summer house band assignment at a local club in Flagstaff. It was a peaceful time in the high country of Arizona. The bandstand provided the mind with demanding responsibly, and the radio station kept the PTSD demons at bay.

GLEN GARY COUNTRY CLUB

"There came a savior in the form of sport".

It would be difficult trying to define any one incident when golf actually became etched or engraved or a part of my soul. When I first began playing golf, there were some humbling moments at the driving range. But winning my hometown 2011 Men's Club Championship at 64 years old was the big payoff, for sure.

The sport literally saved me mentally so many times. Much enjoyment came from searching out a spur-of-the-moment tee time with my good friend Michael Fennello. Sometimes we played early mornings before the sun came up. Other times it was a mad rush at sundown to squeeze in 9 at the local muni. Golf kept me grounded. In fact, I still believe playing by the light of the moon is a great experience.

There were so many times when things were just not going well. After combat deployment, the rejection of being a soldier in an unpopular war always hovered. There were many sleepless nights often followed by a very early tee time. I believe the love of this game helped me after my combat tour more than I realized at the time.

Just after Vietnam and the Marine Corps, my wife, son, and I found ourselves living in Oklahoma City. My second job of playing drums 2 or 3 times a week in a five-piece country band was very therapeutic. I quickly understood that just putting me in an atmosphere of non-rejection helped. To be accepted as the drummer in one of the city's popular country music shows healed many of the earlier negative experiences. My day job at the time was pumping gas at a local filling station while looking for radio work.

This was just shortly after my current wife decided it was time to move from Phoenix back to her home in South Carolina. I reluctantly moved mom into an assisted living arrangement and off we went. We got as far as an early family acquaintances place in Oklahoma City before running out of money.

My son Kenneth was almost two years old and things were looking up some. I was also job-hunting and doing auditions at radio stations to further my career as a disc jockey. We had just relocated from Arizona where I had been successful as an afternoon drive-time jock at KHAT AM Radio, a country music station in Glendale, Az. owned by Ray Odom.

One day in Oklahoma City while driving around looking for radio work, I passed this golf course called "Glen Gary C.C.". "Hey that was my on-air name as a radio jock in Phoenix now how odd is that?" So, I decided to unwind a little and play 9 holes of golf. I had just enough time to squeeze in a round before I was due home for supper. I checked into the clubhouse and they found me a game with 3 older gentlemen as they were turning on the back nine.

Etiquette and proper course management came naturally after caddying many times in my youth at the different country clubs back home for Weldon Love and his friends. Now I kept to myself, struggling not to hold up play. I could count the decent shots on one hand and took every "give me" they offered on the greens.

The landscape and placement of trees, bushes, bunkers, hills and lagoons began to explode in vivid detail as the sun started getting low. A game with-in a game began to take shape. I knew it to be a friendly place, but while negotiating the track course my mind was acutely aware of the ambush sights available. It seemed the game of survival was so etched in my daily routine it affected my ability to just relax.

At some point in the round, I began to realize how little effort I had been giving to just winding down, taking life a bit easy and trying to enjoy the ride. Only a few short years from the combat zone, my current task of being a provider was a full time job, and my ambition for success was a another full time job.

Each morning I would bounce up to prepare for the day. It was as if I had to prove to everyone that I could make it in spite of the Vietnam War. Ok, I too can brush it under the table like an insignificant crumb of history. I never brought it up and people never asked. I grew my hair longer so it would be in fashion and I learned to never mention my recent tour of combat.

Even though I was playing with three other gentlemen, I realized I had no clue how to communicate with them. I know now that, at that time, I had still not regained the ability to make friends. In a combat zone, soldiers often got the point of thinking there was no reason to get to know someone when they could be gone the next day. I was still living with that mindset. In a lifetime yet to come I would realize that inability will not dissipate anytime soon. A combat solider completes assignments and keeps his mouth shut. You say yes sir and don't look your superiors directly in the eyes.

It took many years to understand that when this routine carries over to civilian life, it becomes a very negative thing. In time your boss notices, and so do co-workers. They talk about it and tell everyone to be cautious because there is something just not right. One of the most consistent complaints I remember back then was "you are just way too serious". Of course, my explanation was always, "Shouldn't you be?" Striving for success is stressful.

During this time, lighthearted dialogue from people around me just seemed like uneducated garble. Jokes would just zoom over my head. How many times did I hear, "Wow, you just don't get it." Hell, I got it, but why did people interject crap like that when life and success was so much more important. I didn't see any point in doing anything but proceed to the objective!

In thinking back, it was basically hard to relax after exposure to combat and the discipline of military life after four years. When the bell finally did go off and I realized how offensive my demeanor was to some, it was too late. A few of the real true friends hung on during those years. But when you join the service at 18, then spend years at various duty stations, just how many friends can you have when you get home?

It must have been a subconscious pattern to jump into professions that only required distant relationships. Radio work, Sales, Construction and oh yes, music.

Music is something else a person can share with words or movement. It's a place that satisfies your soul while at the same time it creates a space in which you can comfortably communicate. After all, it is a space you can control, a place that is safe. While interacting with the players around you or the zealous audience, they could not see the distant thunder. They could not feel the memory and torment war produces. The shield at the foot lights created a sense of safety and a reason to be different and an excuse to be distant.

You could tell these three new golf partners were having a great time. They were joking although becoming serious while betting on every shot that would bring a challenge to each of them. They were hitting it straight down the middle consistently while I was all over the course taking 7's, 8's and 9's. We hardly spoke for eight holes as I observed the camaraderie they enjoyed. Then walking to the 9 Tee-Box one gentlemen asked if I'd ever had a birdie before. Of course I had not and relayed the truth with a bit of sadness and disappointment.

They had been good-natured while tolerating my play and appreciative of my courtesy while quietly playing along. The jolliest of them said, "Hey young man just keep playing, you'll get one sooner or later". Then I teed it up on our final hole hitting the best drive of the day about 200 yards down the middle on this par 5 home hole.

Just as their confidence in me started to build a miss-hit on the second shot about 50 yards further down the fairway happened. They immediately left me to my anguish as I walked after it. Now I'm faced with a 200-yard shot over a pond with traps in front of the green. Even though at this point pulling off a shot like this was about 1 in a 100, I decided to go for it. Just to get it on the green, and even have a putt at the birdie would make my day.

As I addressed the ball things began to happen in slightly slow motion. My last look at the green two football fields away came with squinted eyes. The last thing I remember seeing before I pulled the trigger on the backswing was a few birds feeding on the fresh thrown seed on the green.

The ball sailed as if being shot out of one of those howitzer cannons I spent time with. How could that be as it felt like I swung to slow? It climbed high into the setting sun while my voice uncontrollably said "wow" watching it sail towards the green. It was headed towards the right side putting surface. I hoped it would land soft and not roll off the backside of the green. Lucky for me, but not for the bird's head that it landed directly on, the ball kicked sharply left and was pin high about 3 or 4 feet away from the cup.

The large black bird died instantly without a bit of suffering. The curse was broken; I made the putt for a birdie at the cost of a real bird. The three golfers never said a word as I carried the lifeless body to the side of the green. Here it would rest until the grounds keeper arrived to give it a proper fair well.

We were shaking hands in the parking lot after loading up our clubs. It was easy to sense that I had somehow scored a very unconventional first birdie. Not one of them wanted to congratulate me on the score. The only line I could come up with was, "So, what do you call that, "A Double Birdie"? You could tell they were not that amused. But they were polite and said, "We hope to see you out here again" Gary. What was your last name? I told them that was my last name and my first name was Glen. With the golf course being Glen Gary Country Club I could tell they thought I was being very sarcastic as they walked away without saying another word.

Not wanting to leave them with that final thought, I reached for my wallet, walked over and said, "Hey guys, if you ever need a fourth please give me a call. I leaned forward, extended my arm and handed them a KHAT Radio card with Glen Gary as my on-air name printed on it. The Phoenix phone number on the card had to have eventually become obvious and I hoped they realized I had given them the card so they wouldn't think I was just being a smart ass.

It was here in Oklahoma City shortly after that round of golf that my first wife dropped the bomb on me one morning as we woke. She wanted a divorce and that was final. In a matter of 4 hours I packed a few belongings and off to Phoenix I drove. Somewhere in Texas I thought, "What Just Happened"? So I stopped and made a phone call. Aunt Dorothy told me that my mother had just passed away and they were expecting me as soon as possible to return to Phoenix.

Now, I had just finished a tour in Vietnam, spent four years in the Marine Corps and then, while driving back to Phoenix, my mother passed away. It took a few weeks for things to start coming back into focus. I had no clue what I was going to do. Having no siblings, or close family support I withdrew within myself.

One thing for certain in my life was the golf course. It offered a place to release aggression while gaining small morsels of accomplishment one hole at a time. I started caddying on the PGA tour as often as possible.

Pebble Beach is a dream come true in the eyes of one who takes the tradition of golf to heart. I read everything I could get my hands on during my caddie era. Anticipating a conversation with a pro over a cold beer would happen one day, I knew I would need some foundation and history to earn a chance to fit in.

One year I secured a bag for the Phoenix Open with the Minnesota golf pro, Tom McGinnis, at the Phoenix Open. He was only an alternate, but when a qualifier dropped out due to illness we were in. I was finally inside the ropes and now I needed to help this pro make a paycheck.

As soon as the fourth round was complete, he asked if I would like to continue at the famous tournament in Carmel, California at Pebble Beach. It was the next stop on tour so without hesitation I began the preparation to make the trip.

I had been working construction and had a little money saved up so I prepared to catch a flight over to Monterey Bay, California. After arriving at the course and asking some questions about the life of a tour caddie, it all came into focus. Guidance to the right motel and where to check for the Tee Time for my pro prepped me for the evening. I jumped into a poker game a couple of rooms down that evening making a few bucks.

It rained all day that Monday so there was no play allowed. Tuesday afternoon the weather broke some and we got to practice on 9 holes at the sacred Pebble Beach golf course. The rain had washed out a couple of fairways and some other areas of the famous course had taken a real beating. It rained all night again so the Pro Am portion of the show on Wednesday was cancelled, as well.

I checked with my pro that evening and it did not look promising. The consolation prize was an invitation to go have dinner and hang out with him and some friends. Billy Kilmer, former Quarterback of the Redskins, was with us for dinner. The evening was much fun with jokes and laughter continuing until early on Thursday morning.

When I woke and made the caddie shack phone call Thursday morning, I was told the first round had been cancelled. In fact, I was told the course was in such terrible shape they were even uncertain if the tournament would be held this year. Not what I needed to hear. It rained and rained hard until about noon when I finally made a decision. I packed my bags just ahead of check out time and caught a cab to the airport.

The flight landed in Phoenix after sun down and I made my way back to the house. I remember feeling a bit exhausted and discouraged that I even spent that kind of money to get over there. I made a couple phone calls that produced some construction framing work the next morning so I fell asleep early.

It's a Friday now, so the hard day's work in the Arizona sun as a carpenter can sometimes feel like a good ass whooping. I took a shower, turned on the TV and caught a nap on the living room floor.

What woke me up during the evening news was nothing short of a night mare. It was the commentator at Pebble Beach interviewing Tom McGinnus. He said, "So Tom, did I hear that your caddie left you on Thursday?" "Yes" my caddie left", said the familiar voice. I opened my eyes and focused on the interview. As they continued talking it soon became apparent that Tom was leading the Pebble Beach tournament by one shot.

I listened in complete horror when I saw another caddie standing behind my pro smiling. They continued discussing the situation explaining the tourna- ment had been shortened to 54 holes that year because of the rain. Since he had played Pebble that day, he now only had to hold onto to the lead at Cypress Point and Spy Glass for the win. All I could think about was that my chance for fame and a possible career were now blown. I was sick to my stom- ach all night long while truly believing I might not ever recover from this disaster.

As it turned out, Tommy did not have a good 36-hole finish so he collected a very small check and rode off into the sunset. I never saw his name on the lea- derboard or saw him make a PGA cut on tour after that. Of course, my thoughts since that week have always been that if I had been there, could I have made a difference?

What that whirlwind week did for me was a real eye opener and created an important, very long term mind set. During that week, I had been able to forget the Vietnam War. No one talked about the raging killing fields thousands of miles away in those 2 weeks of the Phoenix and Pebble Beach tournaments. Better yet, I never thought about it either. I was swept away in the good life. This was how the rest of the world was dealing with the nightly newscasts. It was Vietnams "American War", and not necessarily a topic of concern with the United States population.

It was as if the war was not happening to their country's youth. Just like the civil rights movements going on prior and currently, it was other people's prob- lems as long as their families were not involved. The war continued on month after month then year after year. If I did voice my opinion on the war, no one wanted to hang out with me.

I silently watched other combat Vets return with major issues. I decided there was only one way for me to survive now. I had to completely immerse myself in my passions and goals. I did construction 5 days a week, played music at night sometimes 6 nights per week and played golf every chance I got.

The intensity of work, music and golf were often met with disapproval by some. Keeping just a few close friends during those following years became a miracle in hind sight. On the surface it seemed I was the ultimate social hybrid but in reality even when I was mingling at a comfortable level, it was staged and forced.

If not for a couple of really good friends who understood my personal demons, it might have continued that way. It took years and years with no counseling for me to feel comfortable around new acquaintances. My personal library is stocked with self-help books. I knew I had to heal to survive, but had no one to tell me how to do so.

When we, or any nation, send their youth to war, there needs to be a mandatory program to help support soldiers when they return home after the trauma of battle. This should also extend to his or hers family support system so they will be able to understand what these warriors are dealing with upon their return.

Most combat Veterans who have achieved a measure of success have done so only because they seem to have found the formula for their survival.

CONSTRUCTION IS THE NEW BATTLE FIELD

One of my first impressions of the job site reminded me of the recent preparation for digging in. A defense position, offensive advantages, storage, escape route when the attack came. It seemed busy with all the usual suspects. Digging trenches, building roads and the teamwork all seemed to make sense.

I smiled at the opportunity to apply my leadership abilities acquired from the Marine Corp. It was now home; Construction, this is my new battlefield. One could distinguish workers by the type of tools in their bags. This was similar to the solider carrying the weapons that defined his job.

There were scared faces uncertain if they were being productive. Seasoned veterans watching out for their trades position on the production front. The commanding officers being the Project Managers, Developers, Lenders, Inspectors, Architects, Engineers, and Consultants. They all had an invisible rank on their lapels that only a few could see. It all made perfect sense from day one.

Above all, the Marine Corps teaches leadership with a take charge or be killed attitude but always with the chain of command in perspective. The recent training from a GI Bill program paved the way for consideration of employment. I completed a 4-year, 3-nights per week class schedule while raising a family. There was a price, and of course it's called divorce. I managed the AA degree in Construction Technology embracing the opportunity with conviction. My three close friends that had family in leadership positions at the famous Sun City in Arizona gave us another opportunity. The well-established company was Dell Webb.

My friend's uncle John Meeker had worked hard to achieve President of the construction company. He was tuff and demanded excellence as his mentor Dell Webb must have required from him. After all my close network of friends completed their tours in Vietnam we became known as the Phoenix party animals.

John Meeker showed up early one morning busting through the front door and saying, OK this is enough. The hangovers were heavy but the respect jumped forward as he explained that we needed to get down to the local carpenters union and sign up.

After some time of digging swimming pools, playing music, and working radio disc-jockey jobs I also soon found myself being dragged out of bed early one morning. It was a union sponsored carpenter's apprenticeship program consisting of 3 nights a week school, and 40 hours a week of on the job training. I was assigned class liaison as well as the Del Webb construction company apprentice safety rep. The four-year program forced me to hunker down deep with commitment just like the previous four years in the Marine Corp. This was my cup of tea, construction I could understand.

It was hard work, in the sun, heat and demands of tremendous production schedule's fueled by the retirement demographic heading west. Turn keying up to 16 houses a day, along with shopping centers, golf courses and infrastructure. Having a truck and radio eased the manual labor program in a short time, and it became all about schedules and coordination of troops, only now it was work force. In a few short years, and one wife later the good money arrived. More than I had ever made in my life. It came in regular salary, large bonus checks, and very often.

A few years later I watched number 3-wife snatch everything away in a heartbeat with no warning. I then understood I needed to start a regiment of aggressive savings. To do this I started ironing my money before depositing it in a savings account. I know it sounds strange, but it was the only opportunity I had to instantly see the benefits of my hard work. It grew fast, and before I knew it 7 years as a single man had sailed by. I pulled out my 401k just in the nick of time before a major stock adjustment gripped the investment industry.

That sixth sense thing happened again that morning before the sun came up. I bolted straight up out of bed after hearing a voice that said "Go Get Your Money". It was so prominent that I could not return back to sleep. I'm thinking OK, T. Rowe Price should open in a few minutes back in Dallas, and I will request my investment be pulled out and mailed.

After asking for my money from the lady on the other end of the phone for some time it became frustrating. It was obvious she was reading from a set of rules trying to talk people from pulling their assets. She said how about borrowing from your account, and dialogue like this was really pissing me off so I asked for her superior. It took two more people before I finally got through to a gentleman that understood how determined and serious I was about them sending me my money.

The check came in a few short days so I went to my bank and opened another account that could be used as a corner stone for my own construction company. Less than a week later the stock market Tec bubble hit, and all of my friends lost at least 75% of their portfolio while they were sleeping one night. I felt extremely fortunate and again had to shake my head about the whole sixth sense thing.

I then studied very hard and passed the Arizona General Contractors test. It was an exceptionally aggressive testing procedure. There were at least 200 questions about the trades, and just fewer than 200 questions about the business side of contracting. The bank eventually gave me a 3 million dollar line of credit while I bonded up, and began bidding projects. Pacing my agenda became very important because I was already at the age of caution. It's the risk factor coupled with, if something went wrong could I recover syndrome.

My son Kenneth had become efficient at painting houses so I approached him about coming along for the long haul and let's make some real money. It all seemed fine at first for him but he was already used to having wads of cash bulging from his pockets. Seeing it grow in an account vs. living off of a weekly allotment did not sit with him. He pulled away and went on his own after some really good paying and profitable jobs. There were times his part would net him about $1,000.00 per day. But he wanted it in his pocket at all times. Seeing the future was only a few days in front of him at best. I never held that against him because of his survival practices growing up in his mom's custody until 15. Ken had been taking care of himself for a long time at that point.

Before long my son did a tailspin into drugs and found himself on the streets at the bottom of society's food chain. We went through a long period of no contact or very little. I never gave up on him and continued to try and be there for moral support. I had already been through the tuff love, enabler business so steered clear of helping him sink deeper into the drug world he was already hanging out in.

I watched many combat veterans use drugs to separate themselves from the pain and memories of actions of survival. Hell for that matter I had some problems earlier in life with the same course of abuse. When it happens to your loved ones there is nothing you can do. They have to want the healing themselves so the recovery is controlled by their agenda totally.

I became hardened and demanding with others in the construction industry. I had hit many home runs in multi-family building so had a stellar resume. Often drifting from my own thing to working with other firms on similar projects. The money just kept getting better and better. High profile projects from 30 million and above became my expertise. Downtown Phoenix next to the capitol, downtown Scottsdale, and other deep pocket developers through out the South West hired me to be their lead superintendent.

We are not saying it was easy along this path at all. I had many ugly skirmishes that resembled a battlefield for sure. The successful survival tactics of war and the comfort of a growing nest egg kept me confident or quick to be impatient with incompetence.

I made it clear to all around me that I was in charge of the battlefield (jobsite), and I can get you out alive, (profit) if you follow my lead. The companies that believed in me reaped the harvest of success. While the ones that did not I would just walk away from. I never had time for failure, regrets, or excuses in the profession. When disaster peeked around the corner survival mode set in. Tactical lessons learned in combat were already instilled then implemented with successful results.

Close observation of drill instructors and leaders in the Marine Corps gave me plenty of ammo. Schedules are purposely aggressive so certain personality types become distraught when they are not met. There would be a field schedule, a company time line, then a bank schedule. Keeping them all straight and rolling in sequence can be mind boggling at best. I never hesitated to use booby traps affectionately known as blue print discrepancies to keep things in perspective.

One of my favorite memories of leadership control came at the cost of a hot headed concrete foreman one afternoon. He had just plowed through 3 of my seasoned assistant supers in a short time. They all came into my field office trailer with looks of despair on their faces. Telling me he had threatened to pull off the job and never come back. He was going to call our office and complain about us. He was about to stop production when we needed an inspection first thing in the morning. To complete his event would allow residents to move in over the weekend.

By the time I got over to the area the man had so much adrenaline pumping he was literally shaking. He began ranting and raving about the jobsite and the difficulty in accessing the locations where he needed to be. A venting session literally inch's away from my face with excuses and reasons why he was cancelling concrete trucks went on for 5 minutes.

When he was finished I began to speak in calm but strength supported tone. I asked him if he was going to be comfortable with failing today. I reminded him he is now going to be required to explain to his boss why the work did not get finished. Then when he got home he will be bogged down with thoughts of failing his assignment that day. He got quiet and started hanging his head low.

I brought to his attention the excuses were weak and exaggerated due to the stressful weather conditions of excessive heat. He would be distraught with shame after a shower and relaxing with his family later in the evening. His mind would be inundated with structuring his reasoning to the boss the next morning. I also mentioned he could avoid all of those circumstances. That the longevity his boss had with our company could be at stake today. He and I both are faced with controlling our emotions and concentrating on the assignment at hand.

My crew stayed late that day as we pitched in and made his event as easy as possible. The sun was setting as I locked up the office and called it a day. Everyone had left with the satisfaction of completing the task. When I arrived at my truck the concrete supervisor was waiting for me. He shook my hand and apologized for the screaming session earlier in the day. The man admitted he felt very good about finishing the job that required completion that day.

He admitted that most superintendents would have let him leave then called his boss to complain and point fingers. We shook hands as I lingered a few extra seconds to wave good evening in his rear view mirror. The rest of the job went smoothly where his production was needed. My team commented to me later about the success of that confrontation.

It was a win win episode for me that time. As we look back on a stressful construction career I have to contribute much to the military foundation received from the Marine Corps. Not saying that all confrontations in my construction career were that successful. This tactic surfaced from memory of a boot camp incident after witnessing a drill instructor help a recruit dig deeper to complete a physical fitness test.

My resume reads over 24 multi-family residential projects taking on the average of 16 months each to complete. Some single family homes and commercial projects along the way were built as well. Money is great to have but the single most accomplished achievement is to live in the home you built. No mortgages or burdens to overcome took dedication and vision. This is as rewarding as completing the 4 years in the Marine Corps, 4 years of Trade School or any other achievement. I've been extremely fortunate and keep that thought as inspiration daily.

How many people do we all know that can start projects routinely, but have so much difficulty in finishing them? It seems being able to overcome this kind of failure always comes back around to survival. Completing a task so the next one can be accomplished is just fundamental vision thought process.

Sometimes actually getting in my way is the overwhelming need to finish something you start. It is like needing to get the task behind me so there is room for other thoughts to stack up for processing next.

I think the one most important legacy to keep intact is your word. Many times I've been upset with myself for saying I would do something. Then not knowing it's complexity until confronted within yourself to do what you say. Of course the byproduct of that is holding everyone else to their word also. A disappointment with others is the perfect way to teach yourself to be impeccable with your word.

In high school I watched my step parents work hard to contract a company to build a kit house. The deal was for me to work the two weeks it took to build the house over summer vacation. It seemed a daunting task when the lumber was dropped on the property all bundled up. The two carpenters that came to put it all together were patient with this 16 year old kid.

They took the time to explain the process while even allowing me to make mistakes along the way. This tactic would serve to embed some real fundamentals about building a house. Things like the different smells of the woods used were remembered. Why pine was used here, but Doug Fur over there became points of topics these craftsmen passed on to me. Their overalls holding certain tools in just the correct places were observed. The prefab and staging events came to light in expert harmony with every progress milestone.

Then there was the afternoon of completion that served to burn a desire that became part of the payoff. They stood back about 50 yards before waiving me over while I was cleaning up the scraps for the day. They stood with accomplishment of a house now, where there was not before. They spoke very few words as their eyes told the story. When they realized I got it, and after starring in silence for some time a check was politely slipped into my splintered hands. They said good job young man, thanks for the help as they drove away.

After all these years the moment we stood back and looked at that little house in Oklahoma is still the big payoff. All of my jobs will be standing many, many years after I am gone. Too list a few of them now is a step back through time with fond recollections. All challenging lessons learned of Survival with a measure of success.

Project Name	Location	No. of Units
San Tan Village	Gilbert, AZ	362
Broadstone @Queen	Creek Queen Creek, AZ	264
Marriott Res. Inn	Prescott, AZ	87
Windsong Apartments	Prescott Valley, AZ	73
Canyon Run Assist.	Living Prescott, AZ	86
Morgan Park	Vacaville, CA	148
Legacy Bungalow's	Phoenix, AZ	200
Alexan Scottsdale	Scottsdale, AZ	246
Alexan Columbia Shore	Vancouver, WA	200
Lions Gate #1	Hillsboro, OR	172
Lions Gate #2	Hillsboro, OR	168
The Colonnade	Hillsboro, OR	272
River Place Town Homes	Portland, OR	168
The Overlook	Bellevue, WA	420
Indigo Springs	Kent, WA	224
Blue Ravine	Folsom, CA	560
Cook Capitol Commons	Rancho Cordova, CA	246
Desert Rose Apartments	Las Vegas, NV	430
Saddleback Apartments	Phoenix, AZ	582

"I WANT A DIVORCE"

Many combat vets have heard these words from women in their lives. More so than the men who have not been in a war zone. I don't claim to have spent hours of research on this subject but it's obvious considering the fact that the man they married is not the man who returns from combat. There will be challenges to which a wife with no combat experience will ever be able to fully relate.

It's all supposed to be perfect; getting back home after discharge from military service and building a prosperous, long and happy life together. How could those wives have known that the demons and memories of war intensify until it is impossible for the veteran to think or act as he did before combat?

Children are born with lack of employment and money will create stress. So many returning veterans have little patience with incompetent leaders and unskilled authority figures. The reality is that over time the man they married evolves into a stranger within the household. How can a wife hang on when their husband won't seek help because he feels that it is a sign of weakness?

My first wife, my son's mother, and I were young when we got married. We met while in Charleston, South Carolina, my first duty station when I got back from Vietnam. We had only been engaged 4 months, which seemed like a lifetime back then, when I received orders to report to Quantico, Va. Marine Barracks up the East coast. I went to her house to tell her I would be leaving the following week. When the day came for me to leave, I pulled away from her apartment and the feeling of separation overwhelmed me. I had only driven about 50 miles before I turned around and headed back. We hugged again and I asked her if she would like to go with me. Her answer was yes, but her family would only approve if I promised that we would get married.

Off we went, filled with excitement about this new life we were going to build together. We found a very nice Justice of the Peace in Fredericksburg, Virginia. The home we got married in seemed small and cramped by today's standards but there was the aroma of fresh bread baking in the kitchen and pastel colors jumped from the window treatments, end tables, rugs and furniture. The frail older couple had the marriage ceremony down to perfection. It seemed like even their smiles were orchestrated. A piano in the corner of the room was silent for our union as we were the only ones there. Everything seemed routine until the gentleman asked how old we were. I was 20 so that did not alarm either of them. When Linda spoke up and said she would be 18 in two months there was silence. The man explained that 17 year olds could not marry in the state of Virginia without a parents signed approval. There was an initial frozen expression on Linda's face until she dropped the bomb. She said, "How about if I have divorce papers with me? The Justice of the Peace said that would be fine. I looked in her direction and said, you never told me you had been married before." She brushed it off as trivial history explaining that her parents had it annulled within 72 hours.

We had a brief history lesson before we pulled out of Fredericksburg that day. It seems that many battle weary veterans came through this town during the Civil War. Most had just experienced a horrific ordeal. In this era, men stood facing each other taking pot shots at moving targets sometimes less than 50 yards away. Very little medical attention was available back then and the hope of survival was slim to none. Thousands of men were suffering with PTSD when they returned to their homeland. I often wondered if our civil war was as avoidable as the Vietnam campaign. Religion, ethical values and forcing the will of a few on the masses is not a recent concept.

Within a year, Linda realized what was in store for her as the wife of a Combat Marine just back from a war. It must have been extremely difficult to live with the PTSD symptoms that were surfacing and, unfortunately, there wasn't any counseling or support system offered back then. I found it hard to believe that many years later she was quoted as saying she never knew I had fought in the Vietnam War. I had learned to suppress those memories as many recently returned combat veterans want to forget their time in combat as if it never happened. Even if she had asked, I probably would not have talked about it anyway.

My self-motivation during this time should be explained. Let me rewind some to set up my work habits. While at our final active duty station I worked 2 part time jobs to save enough money for the return to Phoenix and my desert home. When we did make the move I continued to work as much as I could. I dug swimming pools in the early morning hours and often did a shift as disc jockey at a local country radio station. I also played live music 4 hours a night, for 3 to 6 nights a week.

My mother's health was failing during that period. We moved my mother in with us to save on expenses and I was thankful for each new day we were able to share. Being an only child and knowing I had to support myself and my own family without anyone else to rely on was always on my mind. Looking back, I see I had good intentions. I wanted to take care of my family; in the process my marriage was being destroyed.

Our son, Kenneth, was born at Walter Reed Army Hospital in Washington, D.C. just 9 days prior to my honorable discharge so my wife was taking care of a new baby and trying very hard to understand how to deal with everything that was happening. It was too overwhelming for a young family and the marriage ended.

Within a couple of hours wife number one cancelled our marriage when our son was 2 years old. I was not that surprised to hear she quickly married an active duty Army man. Her new husband had not been exposed to combat and had no symptoms of PTSD. I'm sure she was relieved to know she didn't have to deal with the extreme, obsessive work schedule I had undertaken to help me avoid dealing with PTSD.

I went on to grieve my mother's passing alone. There were many times when regret and the why of it all needed explanation. There were no counselors or VA programs available at that time to help me deal with this major transitional period. I buried the ordeal and moved on with life.

My ex-wife and her new husband had legally adopted my son so he would be eligible for the benefits the military offered, but when they had another boy child my son became the "him" in their family. According to the small bits of information Kenneth has told me, he had to hustle and scratch out a living the best he could when he was growing up. The stories he tells now as a grown man have shocked and saddened me.

When my son's step-dad was discharged from the army, he moved the family several times while looking for employment. They kept their whereabouts a secret from me. They also changed their last name at least twice during this time. I didn't hear from my ex-wife again until they moved from Las Vegas to Tucson when my son was 11.

Ken started running away from home at 12 years old. He searched me out again when he reached 15 and came to live with me in Cave Creek, Arizona at that age. He was just as wild and independent as a desert coyote. He went to work at a local amusement theme park restaurant called Rawhide. When I brought up schooling he said if I forced him to go to school he would run away. Not wanting to see him leave after finally getting him back, I started my own form of home schooling. Kenneth excelled at anything he tried during that time. I was doing construction so Ken worked along beside me much of the time. He took care of the animals and even started working with the stunt men at the theme park as much as five evenings per week.

For two years after wife number one left, life seemed to be a one big party. My mornings were filled with Disc Jockey duties at an FM station KMND Country in Mesa, Az. I was a drummer with a Top 40 Rock band in Scottsdale and that kept the nights exciting. I was burning both ends of the candle and I knew that I couldn't live that way forever. But at the time I still would not admit that there was something seriously wrong and it was causing my extreme behavior.

Those who lived through those times will tell you that the war in Viet Nam and the military that fought in it were being shunned in America by a large number of its citizens. I was shocked at how the American population was reacting to the death and destruction being shown in television newscasts. It was real-time war footage but it wasn't showing what was actually happening in Viet Nam. I quickly became aware that it was best to avoid any conversation about the war, and especially the fact that I had been in combat. I grew my hair long, worked hard, minded my own business and did everything I could to separate myself from the painful ordeal our country was involved in over there.

I tried to create a safe world to surround myself in but I couldn't stop having flash backs about the time I had spent in combat. I couldn't go back to a time before 1966; it was just not there in my mind. I couldn't escape the many horrific visions running through my head hourly, daily, constantly. The close calls, the ugly conditions and smells of war with the sleepless nights. Oh, there is so little sleep in a combat zone, I had brought it all back home with me and it was my normal now.

When I began playing music in local clubs, the popularity musicians received from the crowds were a relief to me after so much rejection. Now I had money, two great jobs and I didn't have any outward signs that I was carrying so much baggage. The club that employed the band I was in became one of the hot spots. There were lines of people waiting to get in wrapped around the building every night. I plowed through women like shucking corn. But I was never able to trust any of them and I did not want any kind of relationship beyond a one or two night acquaintance. There were several who wanted to stay and might have been able to weather the PTSD storm that was intensifying with every passing month. I was surprised at how easy it was for a combat veteran like me to appear normal and "fit in" if he found a way to make a living the public found interesting and acceptable. A veteran could hide all evidence of his service if he didn't talk about it and he never, ever watched a news story about the war. One picture on the news could trigger overwhelming memories.

On the rare occasion when you met a fellow combat veteran there could be small talk about which outfit each had served with. Then silence! There might be an occasional glance at each other. It was like an unspoken language we secretly understood. There were rarely friendships cultivated when combat veterans met because the normal lines of communication were broken. None of us wanted to say or do something that might take the other one back to the combat zone. More than likely it would turn into a "one-up-on-you' blood and guts story fest that could potentially work a combat veteran into a frenzy or a destructive emotional rampage that might lead to suicide.

I had learned that smoking pot insulated me from the memories of war and kept my compulsive workaholic disorder in check. So, when I met the girl who would become my second wife, I believed I was ready to get married again. But the experience taught me one thing for sure. The old saying about beauty being only skin deep is very, very true. She was a cute little thing with a sweet smile and she had a great carefree attitude about life. After a couple months into the relationship, she told me she was pregnant and that would be very disappointing to her father if she were to have a child out of wedlock.

Off to Las Vegas we went on a wild weekend trip. Shortly after we returned it became evident that the marriage was headed for trouble. She had a daughter a short time later and I accepted the child as mine, as well as the responsibility of raising my wife's son from a previous marriage. I decided to make a career change during this time so I could generate enough income to take care of this growing family.

The GI bill allowed me to get formal training and an AA degree in construction technology. It was a long 4-year program of classes but I stuck it out and completed the courses and the carpenter's apprenticeship program. It was really a blessing in disguise when my wife left after only 2 years. She left with the child but came back one afternoon within two weeks. The mother showed up on the front step, handed me the little 2 year old baby girl through the front door telling me she couldn't deal with it anymore. Her parting words were, "You are going to have to take her and raise her". Then wife number 2 with a silhouetted driver hopped in an oil dumping muscle car and drove to California. I didn't hear from her again for 5 years. When she moved back to Arizona we shared joint custody visits for a few more years. That's when the 11 year ole girl by then moved in with her mom who was living in a nearby town. I rarely ever heard from her again after that.

It was soon discovered her daughter had become a heavy drug user and on the few occasions when I did see her, the visits were short and conversations were about the horrible condition of her life. When she started having children of her own without the benefit of a family structure to rely on, I was the one she called when she needed financial help. She gave her 3 children up for adoption just as her mom had and became a street drifter. Landing in jail and being on the streets did not seem to bother her. She was rescued several times from the brink of death only to return to the same lifestyle within days.

A therapist told me I had become her enabler and to save her life I had to stop giving her any financial support. It was hard because I felt like I should but I finally had to admit that the pattern was never going to change and what I was doing wasn't helping at all.

All the schooling I had done was finally paying off and I was making good money but I knew that if I was going to survive the emotional and financial drain she was causing, I had to make a clean break and move on. That decision, in turn, served as her reason to completely abandon the connection with me and she dropped out of sight.

Even though I had vowed to never marry again, I eventually met a lady who was a darn good woman when I met her. She did not want any children and she seemed to love music. Her childhood dream was to come west from New York, meet Glen Campbell and marry him. We met while I was playing music at a steak house in North Scottsdale, Arizona. She was well educated, from a good family and seemed wise beyond her age. I was 9 years her senior.

She stayed with me as I continually tried to re-capture the life that now seemed totally destroyed by the war. I played music on the road and worked nights for many years. Her life as a waitress in a very popular steak house kept her active and involved with people which helped her deal with my neglect as I chased my own musical dreams. Not that we didn't have good times. We had many and she enjoyed meeting many of the country music stars I worked with during our time together. We spent a total of 12 years together and were married for 5 years.

In order to make good money I had to be on the road. I'm sure this must have been one of the reasons she decided to move on. This did not bother me much because by this time I had learned how not to love anyone.

Looking back, I realize my PTSD symptoms were influencing everything I said and did. At the time, I believed I was in complete control of my life. Having to always be in charge and never putting me in a compromising position would soon start playing a big part in how my life was playing out. My attitude could be more easily overlooked at work but not in a marriage.

Music had started taking a back seat to construction again so my wife and I decided to sell the house in town and build a ranch house on a 2 ½ acre property with horse privileges in Cave Creek, Az.

The move was a major undertaking and there were many sacrifices made just getting moved in. During the process, I learned that because my first wife had walked out on the home we bought with my G.I. loan, it was legally in my name only. The house we had built while I was married to wife number 2 was, by law, half hers.

Like music, construction had started keeping me away from home for long periods. I had taken a good superintendent job building apartments in Las Vegas and would only get back home on the weekends. When the ATM machine ate my debit card one evening just after I had made a large deposit from a "hidden-for-many-years" stock portfolio my mother had left me, my gut feeling told me it was not a good sign.

A phone call home confirmed yet another failed marriage and it was quite an eye opener for sure. I immediately started driving the 5 hours it took to return. The drive gave me time to digest the reality of the request for a divorce. Then I began to peel back all the layers of fault, guilt, detachment, control issues, and survival tactics on my own. With this almost obsessive need to succeed and win the war on war, I knew I was going to have to make some changes. There will be a need to change especially if my life ever hoped to have any happiness and peace in the future.

After arriving back to the house at 40 years old, and a mortgage-free residence that I loved dearly this calmness came over me. It became very evident that there was no hope for this marriage when a 6'8" sheriff was on the front porch telling me I had to leave. In fact, I only had a few minutes to gather my necessities and vacate the premises. My only question to him as he put his hand on my shoulder and started guiding me to the driveway was, "Isn't this a civil matter?" He said it wasn't a civil matter in this case because I supposedly posed a physical threat. When one person in the marriage takes those kinds of drastic steps to sever ties, you can believe me, IT'S OVER!

As the officer directed me to my truck he whispered unforgettable words. "Gary, just walk away you can do this all again, she can't." As I waved goodbye from the driveway my last words to number 3 were, "Why does it feel like I just hit the lottery?"

I did not go back to the house right away and by the time I did get there she had hocked all my musical equipment, personal property, tools and anything else of value. Before I had even had a chance to rebound, all of my worldly possessions had been liquidated. I lost almost everything that was dear to me. Her only response was that her house was not a storage facility. The entire time it took to process the divorce I paid the bills for her to live there as well. The state reminded her that the house was half mine and she had to split the sale with me. The fact that I could be ousted from my own home without equal rights to real and personal property left me with disgust for the system greater than anything else I've experienced in my lifetime.

The ranch house sat on 2 acres of land. I begged her to let me have the other acre plus some cash to call it even. She would have none of that and only wanted to cash it all out. Wife number 3 got her real-estate girlfriend involved and they did a quick sale of $70,000 dollars to a lucky buyer. The property was worth $140,000.00 so there might have been some shady moving of money in play.

I welcomed a different state of mind and moved on emotionally. I took the 35k split realizing I probably wasn't breaking even considering the time and hard work I had invested. I had also used up all the special favors all my friends owed me for working on their places over the years. But I was good with it. After all, it was a hard but important lesson learned. It was now time to rebound. I had a good job and I was ready to take advantage of the opportunities before me.

I went the next 20 some years without even considering another marriage. I spent a good portion of that time with a good person. She was energetic, funny, a hard worker and fit every need as a great companion. My reluctance to marry again never got in the way because she wanted none of that either.

By this time, my PTSD symptoms were very prevalent. Stay in charge or be killed ruled everything I did and every decision I made.

As I look back, no other woman comes close to understanding my needs like the lady who became my current wife. She can stand up to a good argument or be as compassionate as a saint. We often talk about how we both had to go where we've been to get to where we are.

Just recently the unit I served with in Vietnam had a casing of the colors disbandment ceremony at 29 palms, California. The 3'rd Battalion, 4th Marines is a unit that has often been put to rest and brought back during times of war. My wife and I made the trip and were both proud of the fact that I had once been a part of such a decorated and heroic Marine Corps battalion.

We were seated with former members of the 3 / 4 in the grandstands. The small talk reminded us that these were the young men we had seen pull down the Saddam Husain statue on the nightly news cast some years earlier.

After taking in conversations from the generation of Marines in front of us, one young man caught our attention with an embittered reply when his friend asked him what he had been up to since his discharge. After an intense moment of silence the young man finally said, "Besides losing most of my hair and going through 3 wives, there is not much to talk about."

My wife squeezed my hand as we both came to realize the same problems I had been dealing with for years still existed with combat veterans. There was none, or very little help for veterans of the Vietnam or the Iraq wars at this point.

I stood with the Vietnam alumni beaming with pride at the company we were keeping that day. There was plenty of silence, a feeling of unity and safety among all of us in the bleachers, as we realized this common bond.

My wife Tina has taken an aggressive approach to understanding all she can about former combat veterans. If your reluctant to commit, or afraid to make a change, don't be. There is plenty of help at the VA these days. A huge shift within the military now recognizes PTSD and the critical need to support combat veterans living with the disorder. You may seem to be okay with everything now, but the memories will surface with vengeance years later. Take advantage of all the help the VA offers post war veterans.

We have now taken an aggressive approach to understanding all we can about former combat veterans. Forty-Five years after my deployment, a VA counselor was more than willing to talk to the wife and myself both separately and together. Without his help, I'm sure we would not have gotten married. I would still be the demanding control freak with reluctant feelings about sharing a life.

Offering my story may show how devastating and uncertain life can be. But I am proof it is never so much that it can't be overcome. Sure, it's depressing and change can be hard. Just keep in mind that America has produced many combat veterans who have weathered their storms and made good lives for themselves.

There will probably be emotional scars and broken marriages and disrupted families. It is not uncommon by any stretch. Remember, with help, it will all work out for the best. Just don't panic and don't give up. I know, easier said than done.

I just had a great conversation with a friend who recently spent 3 extended civilian work assignments in Vietnam. He is a great musician and a Harley Davidson mechanic who has been contracted to start up franchises in that country. Being half my age and certainly of the next generation, I posed a couple questions to him.

I asked him what the Vietnamese people he interacts with now think about America's past involvement in the war with their country. He answered with what appeared to be solid, firsthand knowledge. He said he and other Harley Davidson employees have spent time in the heart of the now modern cities like

Saigon, Da Nang, and Hanoi and they meet and talk to many locals. On several occasions this very topic surfaced while they were out mingling with respected business folks. In every case it was explained that Vietnam has been at war with many different countries for over 400 years. They have been occupied by all the bordering countries, plus Australia, France, China, Britain and many more. America was just another bump in the road. They have no hard feelings towards America at all. In fact, it leans more towards the opposite. They love our products, clothes, cars, music, culture, movies and all of it. There are many American's in Vietnam who has never experienced prejudice or discomfort.

So, almost 50 years after the fact, there is little more than an occasional War Museum that even remembers the war we fought over there. Shocking? Oh, hell yes! You mean we lost over 58,000 men over there and the Vietnamese people just barely remember? My friend Danny Wilson's take on the matter is that we Americans have a much bigger hang up about the war than the people of Vietnam do by a long shot.

It all comes back to the politicians and lobbyists who were in office and who sowed fear and discontent during those times. There were other methods used prior to war to stir the people up. The movie industry had a major role as did the media and toy manufactures. It was all done to entice America's youth to run off to a foreign land and save their generation from certain destruction. It was done to justify the greed of special interests and realize huge financial gains in their own portfolios. What wars were ever truly justified? Did the Wars of 1812, Spanish American, Cuba, WWII, and Korea do any good for the world order in general? History has not done an adequate job in answering this question.

Every country around the globe that has been involved in war has its PTSD victims. Is it dealt with in the same way? The Grey Hairs (popular term at the time) from 1815 were the first to go to congress and demand compensation for saving Charleston harbor from the British some 50 years prior. They got it to the tune of $5 per month. Our political system will give aid to the brave men and women who fought on foreign soil. They just have to demand it.

Just back from combat had enough to buy a 1960 Chevy Impala with wings ready to fly.

Finding myself with nervous energy hiking down and back up the Grand Canyon.

Birthday Party 1953 with Moe & Johnny Love, friends that went to Vietnam together.

A year of VA counseling paid dividends with Tina and good friends Ron & Renee Keel.

Sitting in our family car below the Papago mountains in Scottsdale, Arizona 1952

My father Army officer Lawrence Clemmons sometime prior to my birth.

A rare photo of mother somewhere in Florida around 1947.

Gary Love & I, Vietnam together, then successfully managed a demanding construction career.

Owning and caring for horses helped keep the mind at ease during a PTSD awareness era.

MY 4th house built, this one had NO mortgage, a lifelong ambition and achievement fulfilled.

One of over 24 multi-family projects built from Seattle to Scottsdale during a 20 year period.

PTSD never stops nagging. The Golf game has been a blessing and constant companion.

Just back from the Wall in 2011, SW Airlines Hanger w/ Tina and oldest granddaughter Samantha

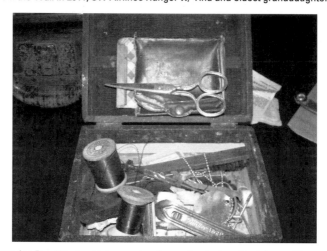

The Box contains Pearl Harbor history and a glimpse back at my Uncle's sacrifices with PTSD.

Landing in Washington DC with Marines I served with in Vietnam

Wedding with most of the family and friends Ron & Renee Keel.

Chaplin Beach who I served with in Vietnam some 48 years earlier. Famous quote in book.

My musical prodigy grandson lost in a car accident at the age of 14 while with his father.

My father home on leave after WW II

My mother fishing off the pier somewhere in Florida late 40's.

"THE BOX" AND "THE WALL"

The Box

It was 1966. I was experiencing a mini-meltdown in the combat zone one day. After numerous days with hardly any sleep I had been working hard in the relentless, overbearing sun and pulling guard duty during long, spooky nights. Depression had set in as the stories kept filtering in from patrols and through field operation dialogue that another soldier had fallen. New information about fellow Marines regularly flowed through the company.

There were a few attempts through correspondence with the war department trying to retrieve some information about my Uncle Kenneth's death while he was in the Navy. Finally while in Vietnam a letter arrived that said there were no records of him being killed while stationed at Pearl Harbor during World War II. That is what I had come to believe all my life.

I wrote a letter home that my mom sensed had a different tone. It had prompted her to call the Marine Corps Chaplain state side. He, in turn, got word to my division in Vietnam. The division commander dispatched a couple of Marine chaplains my way. It had taken about 10 days after Mom told them of my depressed letter I had mailed to her. By that time, I was over the stress of the work schedule, had started sleeping better, and was using positive thinking to control the depression. The chaplains explained that they had been sent to follow up with me. They then began telling me a very condensed version of how my Uncle was killed. They told me he had been murdered in the late 40's while stationed at the naval shipyard in Jacksonville, Florida. They did not have the details, but told me I should do more research when I returned to the States.

I had told them the main reason for my depression was that my Mother had not been truthful with me when she told me my Uncle had been killed at Pearl Harbor.

At the time, blaming my mother for lying to me was the only release for my disappointment and frustration. I was an only child who had no father figure while growing up and I wanted to grab on to some sort of family military history I could be proud of. Years later after receiving the box, I found out my uncle was on the USS Nevada at Pearl Harbor and was wounded in the leg.

He spent some time at a military hospital and was then transferred to Jacksonville, Fl. He was in the harbor that December day in1941. He was a hero and here was my family legacy. The actual reason he was murdered will never be uncovered. I do believe it was a form of and direct cause of PTSD symptoms. The ordeal those sailors must have witnessed during that attack few men will ever understand.

For many years, while my Grandfather was alive, I asked him for a memento, something tangible that had belonged to my Uncle. I would never get a response from him. I later learned from other residents in that neighborhood on La Goma Ave. in Mill Valley, California for years my step grandmother, or "the ole' lady, as they called her, sat by the mailbox everyday waiting for the postman. Helen was Grandpa's second wife and she was going to make sure he would never communicate with anyone from his previous life again.

Our family had suspected that she would gather the mail and screen it before taking it in the house and giving it to grandpa. The letters my Grandpa Wesley was able to sneak out were always filled with affection but sprinkled with an undertone of sorrow. In his letters of apology for the breakdown of family structure he always sent his love along with a check to be put toward my schooling and other things a boy growing up might need.

When I returned from Vietnam and made it to Los Angles International, I called my grandpa and Helen answered the phone. I explained that I had a 30 day leave and I would like to come visit my grandpa for a few of those days. She panicked screaming NO, and told me it wasn't possible because he was back east visiting. I knew it was a lie, but had no stand to call her on it while I watched the phone's black hand piece slip back into its pronged cradle. Sitting a bit longer in the isolated phone booth, I tried to come to grips with my whole family structure. The bi-fold glass door of the booth made a creepy, lonely sound as I opened it and stepped out of the booth. In my mind at the time, I felt the blame for allowing this tragedy to happen rested with grandpa. Consequently, I never knew either one of them on a personal level after I grew up.

Many years later my companion of 15 years, Kim and I discovered that her grandpa was also buried at the same national cemetery as Grandpa Westly in a beautiful setting just outside San Francisco. We decided to go pay our respect and made a day of it by visiting my grandpa's old neighborhood. I got a haircut from the corner barber who said he remembered him distinctively. Kim and

I went to the care facility where grandpa had spent his last year. We stood on the patio outside what had been his room and stared at the trees and grounds. I silently asked forgiveness for not just forcing his wife, Helen, to let me see him all those years ago. I found out where Helen's kids were living and even did a drive by of the youngest son's house just in case I found the nerve to knock on the door for a chat. After lingering for 3 drive byes' I did not stop.

Ever since I could remember from at least 5 years ole grandpa had sent money every month like clockwork for my schooling. I read each of those letters many times. They were filled with good thoughts, advice and love. He explained that if I answered he might not be able to receive the letters but he always wanted me to know that he loved his daughter Peggy. I wrote many letters to him over the years. When I would get a letter back, I could tell by its contents he hadn't received my other letters. It took many years before I would fully understand the situation.

Somehow, everything that Mother would have left to me was gone. That is except for some stock that mysteriously appeared some 18 years later. She paid $50.00 for it and it was worth 3,800.00 when I cashed it in approximately 1988.

There were 3 houses in the central part of Phoenix gone. Everything my mother had gathered and worked for during her career of working with Arizona Title & Trust, the Frank Lloyd Wright foundation, and as well as some assorted stocks along with any Life Insurance policies had vanished. Everything left was condensed to one single envelope that included a few pictures and letters along with my birth certificate, her marriage license to my father and a will that listed me as the sole benefactor. "There was nothing left", my aunt Dorothy said, while smacking as she chewed her wad of gum during mother's funeral. My Mom passed away shortly after my return from the Military. Her aunt, my great aunt Dorothy, took control of my mom's funeral arrangements. After the small memorial service, she handed me that large yellow envelope. I was stunned and completely distraught from crying for the first time since grade school. I asked no questions other than, "This is it?" Dorothy said they had sold everything Mom had to take care of her cancer operation and all of the other medical bills.

It was 1970 and I was on my own completely without any family what so ever. Aunt Dorothy was distant and unresponsive to any needs I might have had from that time on. I've now returned to a hometown that really didn't know me anymore. All of my friends were still fighting over in Vietnam, married, or had moved on. My second wife was so far emotionally removed, she had never even asked about my family and knew nothing about my past. For that matter, it soon became obvious she had never really cared. There was really no one for me or anyplace I felt comfortable. My recent military and combat experiences were shoved deep down in my memory and I moved on only focusing on survival.

I would like a moment here to fast-forward to a day in 2011 when I opened a letter from California. It was from a concerned lady who explained she had been cleaning out her attic a few years prior and had come across a letter with my return address. In the letter, I had pleaded with the recipient to please allow me to have something, if just one thing, anything at all, that had belonged to my Uncle Kenneth or Grandpa Wesley Krampe. I had explained in the letter that I felt a strong need to connect with my family and that I wanted to be able to pass some family history on to my son. She told me the letter had touched her deeply and had been on a quest to locate me for many years. She asked in her letter if I was indeed the person she had been looking for and, if so, to please give her a call so she would finally be able to fulfill my request.

She explained her commitment to the task and how many letters she had found written by me with various return addresses over the years. I had been working a 25-year construction career by this time, so I had made moves about every 16 months or so. We became very close through our many phone calls and emails. We developed a definite bond, a connection which she needed before she was able to mail me the box. It also became apparent there were some sacrifices and discomforts experienced on her end to accomplish the shipping of "The Box".

It took quite a while for me to get the box of articles, but one day it finally came. It was a large box and I was both excited and extremely nervous. I couldn't even bring myself to open it for over two weeks. But I will say there had been a bad flu season that year so part of that time I had been very sick. I stared at that box everyday thinking back through my life remembering all the times I had dreamed of getting personal items from my family who, by now, had been gone so long.

But the day finally came when I was ready to open the box. Beyond the tightly wrapped tape came the smell of years. A vivid smell that meant I would be learning about the family I really never knew. The box had everything in it I had dreamed of and then some.

It had letters from my mother to grandpa telling him of our love and how she wished we could see him. My grandpa's old shipyard workbench vise and other personal items were there. There was a flag from the USS Nevada, scrapbooks of WW II and many personal items that had belonged to my Uncle. There was a lighter from Pearl Harbor, a personal pocket knife, a uniform, an ID card. The many years of yearning for a connection were all there. I would sometimes just sit and hold one of the items. These were touching stones to the reality that, yes, I came from a family that had served our country in a profound way as I had. This box arrived shortly after I had returned from a trip to the Vietnam Memorial Wall in Washington D.C.

The Wall

After all these years, I found myself on the way to Washington. I was going to the Wall, the Vietnam Wall. The Vet Center said there could be healing there and they hoped me and the others on this journey could find relief from the anguish of war and the memories of the hell experienced so many years ago.

The four-day trip offered much more than any of us could have ever anticipated. The people's response was the complete opposite of what we, the Vietnam veterans, had received when we returned from combat. It triggered a complete breakdown from normal we had been living with for so many years. Even though the healing effects were prevalent, the aftershock, at least for me, was devastating. Shortly after my return from the wall, I plunged into a deep depression. A hell I wish no one ever had to know.

There was great good to be had from the experience, but it took months of therapy and a very good personal coach from the VA to heal the wounds.

These two events, "The Box" and "The Wall", occurred back to back. Each stirred up all the emotions I had managed to keep buried for years. Who would have thought that these two experiences would trigger repercussions that, when worked through, would eventually give me more emotional security than I had felt in decades.

It was revealed later that indeed, a small percentage of the Vietnam War veterans who visit the Wall later in life, experience a mental episode that, at times, could become difficult to control without professional guidance.

Allow me to describe the Washington D.C. trip with words that came to me directly upon my return. My first stroll towards the wall on Nov. 9th, 2011 was not unlike the first walk outside of Hue, Vietnam in Feb. 1966. It was solid cloud cover, misty rain and the air was thick with moisture. Missing was the constant thumping of un-muffled chopper engines as they dropped into the clearings. Missing was the youthful excitement of a new adventure I had felt then. There were now only somber feelings of apprehension.

The 58,272 names that were etched there seemed to breathe life as I walked by each granite slab. Back and forth I went, pacing and glancing at names. Then I started repeating a name over and over in my mind before I moved on and read another name. It seemed that by repeating names this way, it might somehow trigger the memory of a fallen friend.

It had just been hours earlier, just before lunchtime, that me and my fellow vets had been leaving Phoenix on Southwest Airlines. As they had announced our boarding instructions, the amplified voice could be heard throughout the terminal telling everyone there were Vietnam veterans boarding the flight and also mentioned our sacrifice. That's when the entire terminal broke into applause. I felt embarrassed as I walked by grown men with tears in their eyes; the older generations were reaching out to shake our hands.

Children were saying thank you as we passed by. I then overheard one of our trip counselors tell another veteran on this "Operation Freedom Bird", that we hadn't heard anything yet, he was right on!!! Let me explain.

We landed at Washington/Baltimore National airport to another tremendous welcome from other passengers throughout the airport terminal and continued all the way to the waiting chartered buses. We found ourselves showing a little more emotion after a long 6-hour flight. Most of us were acknowledging the recognition and appreciation people were showing us and there seemed to be more handshakes and longer eye contact. The matching ball caps and polo shirts we were wearing somehow seemed to reunite us again after many years. The unity of this forgotten generation of warriors was now established and the bond made as we continued this eastern pilgrimage became a power unto itself.

Upon our arrival at the Vietnam Memorial, there was a long period of uncanny silence as we each began to confront our own private thoughts. Feelings of pain, depression and sadness seemed to have been absorbed into the earth here in this place. The granite stone ranged from 0 to 7'5" high signifying the year 1975 when our troops pulled out of Viet Nam, then gradually decreased in heights until it once again reached ground level. The memorial is tucked between the Lincoln Memorial, Washington Monument, State Department, Reflecting Pond and other landmarks. It quickly became clear to me that the "buck stops here". My amazement had turned into exhaustion later when I was standing below old Abe remembering some of the items families, friends and fellow veterans had left at the Wall in just that one day.

We bussed to the Iwo Jima memorial the next morning and had VIP seating for the Marine Corps Birthday celebrations. I knew the day was going to be special as when the duty station's Sgt. Major strutted towards me snapping to attention and extending his hand to say Happy Birthday Marine!

We carried on a casual conversation, and he thanked me for my service in Vietnam as TV and press correspondent moved through the crowd. I sat next to a 3 star general, a full bird colonial, and a major. The Marine Corps President's Band performed one of the most moving concerts I've ever heard in my life. Guest speakers spoke of the campaigns, the accomplishments and history of my Marine Corps.

At this point, a special guest stepped up to the microphone to celebrate our 236th birthday. Ironically, that number was also my company platoon's number in boot camp at San Diego in 1965. The guest speaker was the latest recipient of the Medal of Honor, Sergeant Dakota L. Meyer. He spoke of the Marines who had come before him and had inspired him and given him the courage to perform what he described as just an act of duty. His citation, as described on the USMC History page online, calls his feat an act of heroism.

That afternoon, we returned to the Wall. We were dropped off with the parting words, "We will pick you up in 5 hours". I thought, as many did, "Oh crap! What the hell am I going to do for all that time?" As it turned out, they had to hunt many of us down to tell us it was time to leave.

It was almost dark and the evening had turned chilly when my personal moment of sudden, overwhelming connection to the past happened. We overheard later the counselors were calling it Wall Magic, but it was much more than that.

I had asked one of the park helpers to guide me to the granite wall where the names of those who lost their lives during my tour, Feb. 66 to December 1966 were etched. As I stood there staring, reading, remembering and reflecting, I must have gotten lost in thought because I suddenly realized my body was pressed up against the two slabs. My arms were reaching out touching every name. The area was packed with people of all nationalities but I saw no one. I just kept silently repeating "It could have been me".

I thought to myself, "Why didn't I ask the names of the smoldering body's I loaded on the choppers? Why didn't I write down the names of the young men like me who had served with me?" A voice inside of me seemed to say, "It's because it's not something we did". Not in war, not when daily replacements were rotating in and body bags were being hauled out. Survival mode became a way of life. Warriors moved on, to the next operation, the next day, the new daily task of staying alive.

Veterans Day that Nov. 11th, 2011, found me in the VIP seating section that had been set up in front of the wall. One of the guest speakers that day was Joe Galloway. Galloway was the war correspondent who took many of the photos's documenting the history of the Vietnam War. Joe also wrote the stories that Americans were not being told at the time. He later made returns trips to Kuwait, Iraq and Afghanistan documenting more harsh realities of war. Galloway has been awarded every honor a Civilian can receive for putting his ass on the line for so many years recording the history of these conflicts. We were his people, Marines he had stood beside in combat zones, who he was delivering the speech to that afternoon.

During that ceremony Rolling Thunder, the biker group of former Marines, walked up and gave Joe Galloway $100,000 dollars to insure the continuation of the "magic of the wall". Before he finished speaking another million dollars was pledged. Upon hearing that announcement, the History Channel pledged another million dollars. These new funds were to be used to build an Historical Building on the grounds that will house photographs of every fallen Vietnam Veteran along with other displays of historic significance. One of the many statements he made during his speech had the strength to get him elected to office if he had wanted to go into politics. That statement has stuck with me. He said, "No Congressman or Representative should be allowed to vote for war, unless he's been involved in one".

There were many wonderful guest speakers at our banquet that night. One who was especially impressive for me was former Vietnam Veteran Hall of Fame Radio NPR host, Jim Bohannan, an elegant speaker with more survival of combat wit and wisdom than anyone I've ever heard.

The Veterans Centers of Arizona, a non-profit organization, has sponsored this trip for veterans for 24 years. Captain Patrick Lynch started the effort and since turning it over to a new generation of Vets from our more recent campaigns. Some of the younger veterans were on the trip in 2011 and it appears to me we have a most respectful and caring generation to take over, aid in and support the healing process for Americans currently returning from combat.

When we touched down at Sky Harbor International Airport Saturday night, the Phoenix Fire Department Water Canon Trucks welcomed us on the taxiway with arcing streams of water. The terminal was filled with family, guests and travelers. We were all rushed to the Southwest Airlines hanger for a welcome home party with entertainment and quest speakers. By the look on the veteran's faces, it was much appreciated.

My family was quiet as we headed away from the airport. Finally a sweet, beautiful child's voice was heard as my granddaughter, Samantha said, "Thank you grandpa". My thoughts were jumping back and forth at the wonder of it all. My survival had made this moment possible. My mind went back to that winter evening in December, 1966 when I had walked towards 12th St. and Indian School in Phoenix, Arizona. I was just back from Vietnam, alone, and I remember whispering out loud, "What the hell just happened?" As I walked from the airport to the car with my family I was reminded of a walk I had made many years earlier. My destination had been a dark, deserted football field at North High School. Again, I had just recently returned from Vietnam. That night my fingers had been grasping the chain link fence until my knuckles turned blue as I reflected on my South Asian tour.

"Hell, "I'm here, go figure," I thought. I'm alive, so now what do I do? I'm alive with no one to share the experience with. The next morning and the days that followed, I convinced myself I had put my time in combat behind me and moved on. But the experience really never leaves you. Not for one day, never!

For years, from that morning on my daily decisions had been made based on the ruthless survival skills I had learned in combat. But my nights were filled with music and if not for that, I too could have been just another suicide statistic.

Soon enough we would all understand that not talking about our experiences would have serious, long-term effects. Without getting help, our problems would manifest and intensify as time moved on.

If anyone has a relative returning from combat, please take the time to welcome them home. Give them support and room to heal and grow through the ordeal. And if you see someone in uniform, it does not take much to say "Thank You" for his or her sacrifice. Society has learned the adjustment period is better confronted now that later.

The suicide rate of returning war veterans has always been at staggering levels. Every war in America's history has produced some of the most outstanding individuals. We read about them from time to time. What we do not hear about is the pain and suffering so many of our veterans endure after they return home. Not only the veterans themselves, but also their families are impacted by the aftereffect of combat on their loved ones.

Society has learned that the adjustment period men and women go through when they return home is a critical time and combat-related issues should be confronted and dealt with right away rather than later. The 21'st century has brought about changes for veterans dealing with PTSD, and it was time.

OPERATION FREEDOM BIRD

Southwest Airline
Gary Kelly
President & Chief Operation Officer
Love Field
P.O. Box 36611
Dallas, TX.

Dr. Mr. Kelly,

As I looked out over our great land from the window seat on our recent trip to D.C. from Phoenix, Arizona, I could not help but be amazed. Your generosity in making it possible for our Vietnam Vets to experience this most profound healing trip is beyond description.

I know that I and many others on the 2011 pilgrimage would never have even thought of making this trip had it not been for Southwest Airlines. Sometimes the need is never fully recognized until the benefits are revealed.

Your employees were all aboard, from the baggage personnel on the taxiways to the boarding staff in the terminals. It was obvious they all share your vision of the need for this wonderful gift.

May your lives be rewarded with peace and comfort as ours have been upon receiving this opportunity. Your compassion for the sacrifices of our combat veterans my friends, is the true sign of champions of patriotism.

Wishing you prosperity and a wonderful future.

Best Regards,

Gary L. Clemmons
USMC 1965 – 69
Sgt. Vietnam 1966
Simper Fi

C-130 ESCAPE TO FREEDOM

From 4th Mar. Hdqs. Co. Dong Ha, Vietnam
December 11th 1966

The time was nearing for my combat zone rotation date. I had anxiously counted each day for months. Three days prior to my departure date, the company clerk came to my hooch and asked if I would mind giving my seat to a Sgt. that wanted to get home in time for his wife's birthday or something. I did not really want to do it, but he promised I would rotate the following week, no questions asked. I reluctantly gave in with a little more persuading.

The day had arrived, I made it, I was alive. We loaded in the C-130 cargo prop plane with some not trying to hold back the tears of joy anticipating the long ride back to the United States. The runway at Cam Lo was made of solid metal sheets with holes all connected together. We strapped in the cargo nets as the pilot taxied out to the starting point. Full throttle, we headed to the other end only to feel the opposite thrust a few seconds later. The pilot explained we were a little overloaded and he needed to try it again.

This time we inched our way to the very end of the runway. With smiles on our faces we were off again with all the Marines lifting there feet and grunting to help the twin-engine bird lift off. Again the pilot shut it down. He turned it around and headed back to the starting point again. This time he came on the loud speaker and said, "Well, men, we are going to give it one more try". Now, if it doesn't work this time, we are going to ask 10 Marines to get off and catch tomorrow's flight to Saigon".

I think we all started praying silently, our heads down. Who was going to determine the 10? Would I now have to get off the plane and spend another night at this last resort landing strip? The pilot remained at the end of the runway for what seemed like forever. Maybe he was waiting for that little gust of breeze that could make all the difference. This time there were no smiles or nervous joking.

The C-130 finally lunged forward with a moan and shutter; someone started shouting, "GO ". It didn't take long until everyone was repeating in unison, "Go, Go, Go!" This time he did not shut it down. When we could no longer hear or feel the metal track beneath our feet, we knew we were off the ground. Shortly, one of the crew members came back to the cargo area where we were all cheering. When the noise finally did settle down he said, "If you guys only knew how close that one was".

As we had boarded this freedom bird, I caught the last glimpse of my war zone. At the end of the runway there was a fighter jet sticking nose first into the dirt embankment. Here was evidence of not being able to stop before the landing strip disappeared. I had seen this oddity many times from ground level but it took on a different perspective this day. With the gentle sway of the cargo net seats, relief started settling my thoughts. We were headed south this time. That thought alone was calming beyond belief.

We weren't told what we would be facing upon our return to the United States. There would be no help with survival guilt or other effects of combat that had been documented in previous wars. These Marines would not be receiving any guidance or information about America's intolerance of this conflict. It would only be a short time before we realized our country did not want to hear about it. As we returned to our neighborhoods and families, many of us would hear nothing but words of resentment for our roles in South East Asia. We soon learned to just keep quiet and suppress the memories. The toughest years of my life were about to become a memory, but it was a memory that would never go away.

One thing for sure, that lift off from deep Viet Nam is etched in my mind like a scene from an old classic movie. A similar feeling would surface many years later while on the approach to Phoenix International Airport.

After my third divorce, one of my best friends offered me a position as a construction superintendent in Sacramento, California. Taking this offer afforded me a new beginning with opportunities I had not even dreamed of. It would end up becoming a 12-year employment tenure with one of the biggest multi-family construction developers in the country. I took full advantage of the opportunity and dove in with commitment and determination.

It had become habit to take a vacation and fly into my hometown once a year to visit my son. Kenny worked at an auto dealership and would plan the delivery of a rental truck to the airport timed perfectly for my arrival. The plane had entered the flight pattern for landing when the decent suddenly felt strange and I felt a surge of un-expected lift. The climb back up to a higher altitude was abrupt and uncomfortable.

The pilot came on the intercom and explained there was a dust storm brewing on the desert floor. For safety, we were going to remain in a holding pattern until it passed. The 707 had held a tight counter clockwise pattern for over 30 minutes when a blood-curdling scream came from the seat right in front of me. I knew that people were scared. It was experiencing that feeling of awareness that had been cultivated many years prior in combat. I was having issues controlling peaceful thoughts as well. Everyone around me had been holding on to the armrests with white knuckles for some time. The stewardess could barely walk down the aisle due to what seemed like a 45-degree pitch the plane had been holding for some time. When they reached the lady, she was totally un-raveled and screaming at the top or her lungs. Her hysteria created even more alarm in the other passengers. I knew those looks all too well. People were scared!

We leveled off and headed for the Tucson airport less than an hour away. We landed there without incident and remained on the plane for another hour before attempting lift off. As we waited in line for the clearance to take off from Tucson, the memories of leaving Viet Nam returned with a vengeance. Every smell, motion and feelings of that ordeal with me in my sweaty combat fatigues came alive again. Those looks on the passenger's faces took me back to that last attempt at the Dong Ha runway. Memories of that late December day in 1966 haunted me for the remainder of the flight back to Phoenix.

I have major problems with flying to this day. Whenever the suggestion or thought of having to fly arises, the memory of that C-130 flight out of Viet Nam will surface. I start creating reasons not to get on the plane, not to go on the trip. I will decide driving is just a better deal.

When the Phoenix airport had announced the delay of my flight, my son had to leave and return to the airport several hours later. When I finally came out of the arrival tunnel, I was more than happy to see his handsome face that so resembled mine when I was in my early 20's. I bit my lip to suppress a slight quiver. At that time, I just wanted to sit down and tell him about that flight from Viet Nam. How, it was only because some of us were lucky enough to survive that war that he and others were even born. We are so fortunate to have each other, I thought. But time and schedules took precedence and we never talked about the flight that brought me home from Viet Nam. To this day, we have never just had a down to earth conversation about my involvement in the Vietnam War. Short, mild-mannered discussions of his parents' divorce are all we have been able to muster from that time period.

Many times since that day in the airport with my son Ken, we have had the opportunity to talk about my being a combat zone veteran. It just never seems to happen. I think we both wonder if it would do any good at this point. It's possibly and to acknowledge what happened could be a cleansing or building block.

Even though this chapter is titled Escape to Freedom, it could be more correct if I renamed it. To what I do not know but I do believe once combat is experienced you can never escape completely. Sure, there is the freedom of physical distance, but not mental freedom. The ordeal is there and it stays, and stays, and stays.

One example of this is when I finally realized how the memories were affecting my life. Yes, I carried a gun. I not only carried one in combat, but also for some time after returning to civilian life. The gun that I bought for $25.00 in Vietnam made it back with me and it was my insurance policy. The under-arm sling and holster became part of me.

My justification for carrying that gun came from one dominant thought. That was that I was not making it out of Vietnam alive just to come home to have some thug take me out. The gun fit comfortably so my body language never gives it away. I learned to stand against walls and never let people walk behind me without keeping a watchful eye. I never, ever sat with my back to the room in a restaurant. To this day, it is the first thing that cross's my mind when I enter a public place. Before any business takes place, one must put together an escape plan.

This is not real freedom. This is hard-core, instilled paranoia. This is real symptom, a disease not un-common to combat or peace keeping participants. Suicides were prevalent among the ranks of vets returning from Vietnam for many years. As for me, it wasn't unusual to find me driving as fast as my car would go down a busy street in the city, running red lights, laughing. Yes I did that many times. I know now it was a death wish but I did not know how to control it.

When I went for help at the VA office in 1969, the clerk said, "Why are you reaching out to us? Hell, you're free, white, and 21 so just go for it man." At the time I thought that was just about the best clinical help I would ever receive from the VA.

I had 2-1/2 years left in the Marine Corps upon returning from Viet Nam and quickly realized that being an only son would prevent a second tour. In those days, if you did one tour they did not necessarily recruit you to return unless it was a volunteer request.

Still being active duty in the military, I knew I needed to provide and survive. I buried myself in daily duties, second jobs off base and extra school credits.

This mentality carried over to civilian life after my honorable discharge. And I still was not without my trusty pistol under my left arm. I was working as a carpenter during the day and playing music 5 nights a week at a local steak house. I struck up a relationship with a beautiful waitress that lasted for some time. She also was swept aside when need to control surfaced. Even at her young age she knew I could not fully commit to a relationship. She knew that if I did, it would make me feel to vulnerable. Some of my friend's, men and women, got that and ran for the hills. Others felt the distance I projected and just drifted away. To see them go was a relief. I'm alive and I survived again.

Some 5 or 6 years later, during an era with a very successful band we called Stumpwater-Jak, a strange and surprising incident untolded. It was in the 80's when the southern rock/outlaw music was popular. We found ourselves with a hit record on the radio and our popularity began to get us plenty of press and notoriety.

One night at one of our bookings I eased up to the bar for a cold beer after the show. The crowd began to filter out for the evening. This young man drifted up and sat down right beside me even though there were plenty of empty seats available. I did not feel like conversation so stayed steadfast and focused on the label of that cold beer. He soon began speaking in what one would consider an intimidating manner.

"Hi Gary, you don't remember me but I was a bus boy at that steakhouse you were playing music at a few years back." I silently acknowledged his presence, turned and began to listen more intently. He explained that I had stolen his girlfriend, used her and then left her with a broken heart. He told me he used

163

to follow me home after work waiting for the right opportunity to kick my ass. I let him get it all out of his system.

By relaying the anguish built up over the past years, he appeared to gain more confidence. It was obvious he was starting to feel good about himself for finally confronting me on the issue. He said a lot more that night but then, as now, most of it was blurred or quickly forgotten. While I waited for the perfect opportunity to speak, by the look on my face he must have seen I didn't give a shit about his need to unload.

When I did finally start to speak, the words came with pure honesty. I told him he might have made the best decision of his entire life by not confronting me back then. Very much in control of my emotions, I explained my combat tour as well as my need, then and now, to carry a loaded pistol with me at all times. The fact that he did not take that opportunity to kick my ass more than likely saved his life. When I finished talking, the expression on his face, although subtle, told me the conversation had abruptly ended. He slowly got off the bar-stool and left the club. I never saw him again after that night.

A few weeks later, in the same nightclub's parking lot, another situation unfolded. What should have been a scary incident seemed to feel insignificant at the time.

Toward the end of the night, a female acquaintance had approached me and said she had been separated from the company she came with and needed a ride home.

I said of course so we headed to my truck. It was a nice summer evening, and I had the driver's side window down. We talked for a short time about where she needed to go. All of a sudden, from my blind side, a crazed ex-boy-friend had a gun pointed about 6 inches away from my head. She started pleading with him to put the gun down and relax. She told him she had asked me for a ride home and that's all there was to it. He had both hands on the pistol and was starting to shake violently.

Her ex pointed the gun at my head for what seemed like 5 minutes. He kept telling me he was going to blow my head off and yelled every other threat that came to his mind. She was afraid to get out of the truck and just continued begging him not to do something stupid. He took an aggressive wide stance and stuck the gun directly between my eyes.

It seemed like a dream as I began to speak. There was no fear, no panic, and no emotion. I said, "Either pull the trigger or put it down. Do you really want to have a gun battle right here? Right here tonight? Is this judgment day? Is this what you want? Make it a perfect shot, make it count", were my orders. I taunted him, even encouraged him. About that time she jumped out of my truck and said, "OK, does this make it better? I'll find another ride home."

I sat in the parking space and my eyes followed him in my rear view mirror. They got in his truck and left. There seemed to be a letdown of sorts. This ordeal was over and the adrenaline was just starting to flow. Acute hearing, vision, rational and accomplished survival tactic had taken over in my mind. I swear the smell of gunpowder was in the air. My feet were hot, and the signal lights at intersections resembled flares on the way home.

MUSIC BUSINESS

After being on the road for many years playing music all over the Southwest, I decided to settle down on 2 1/2 acres in Cave Creek, Arizona. The sale of my first house covered the financing of the investment. I rented a room next door while building the house and lived as if camping for a little over 6 months. The township address was Cave Creek Stage with the nearest store about 6 miles away. Picking up a couple horses offered plenty of enjoyment riding in the new surroundings.

One evening, while riding with good friends, we all noticed a very low-flying, silver plane with no markings right in front of us the look of Air America all over it. We looked over to our left and there in the desert was a brand-new Cadillac with a very short, Italian, black suit, cigar smoking fella leaning on the trunk of his very expensive car staring at us. We looked over to the right and there were two dirt bike guys fully equipped with suits and matching helmets. They were staring at us knowing we witnessed the bails of marijuana that just came from the back door of the plane overhead.

It became obvious that we were in the wrong place, at the wrong time. One of my friends turned around looking a little frantic saying, "We are in the middle of a drug drop. Let's get out of here." He slapped the back of his horse and off he went in a cloud of dust.

All four of our horses went from 0 to 40 in what seemed like seconds. I got dislodged from my saddle and was barely hanging on as we headed full speed through the desert. Sure enough, I could not hang on any longer and I let go of the saddle horn and landed hard in a sea of Cholla cactus. I had to lay there and let my friends pick cactus needles out of me for about an hour.

The entire time while looking up to the sky I was thinking about a Marine I had witnessed get hit by shrapnel just before I left Viet Nam. I had watched the field surgeons carve out pieces of metal while sounds of agony filled the night air in that combat zone. There was one very noticeable difference this time. With every cactus needle plucked, there came an uncontrollable snicker from my friend, Steve Powers.

I had to take a pain pill so I could play a gig that night. Every time I looked at Steve, who was our roadie/soundman, he broke out in involuntary fits of laughter. Steve later tried to explain that he just could not help himself, After seeing me in such a different light the image of me laying there getting those cactus needles pulled out was the funniest thing he had ever seen. He ran sound, lights and became our extra support in the music business for many years. His brother Darrell and many North Phoenix friends supported country music and our projects, in general.

I immersed myself in the music business upon my return from Vietnam. I tried to file away all the horror and destruction I had seen. Music also allowed me to numb the sting from my recent divorce with wife number 1 and the temporary separation from my son.

Doing an early morning disc-jockey show, then hurrying to my apartment for some much needed sleep was the norm for me. Looking back, it's a wonder I was able to sustain health with my life style. I don't remember ever slowing down to eat. Photos justify this as they reveal a very skinny me.

Waking up in the early afternoon and working very hard to learn the new material for the live performance schedule that evening was a daily routine. Music did not come that natural for me. I was fortunate to have many great players who shared space with me on their stages. I remained a constant sponge and always spent an exceptional amount of time rehearsing the material.

We had a show booked at a large club in the central area of Phoenix one evening. The owner sold tickets and it was packed to the rafters, as they say. A good friend brought a camper to the rear entrance of the club by surprise that night. It was my first time ever eating mushrooms and it turned out to be the one and only time. I never did that again.

Back in Vietnam, I was exploring a box that had been dropped in with the daily supplies. It had about 12 dozen lipstick looking containers neatly in a row. Taking one out and trying to figure out what it was eventually triggered a spring loaded needle full of morphine. Much of it went in my thumb, but I was able to squeeze most of it back out of the hole the needle made. Still, in about 20 seconds I went straight back and laid there starring up at the sky for a long time.

When I finally started regaining my senses and focusing in on the surroundings, I saw there was nobody paying any attention. That was fine, because I was too embarrassed to explain what had happened. I was reminded of that experience when the mushrooms started taking effect during the third song in the concert that night.

Jerry Gropp, our lead singer, turned around and looked at me with a smirk on his face. Well, that was all it took. I turned into a laughing hyena in a matter of seconds. Soon we were all laughing so hard we had to stop playing. This went on for the whole night.

I noticed the people who had bought tickets to the concert did not see anything funny at all and just sat there in a state of shock at what they were watching. Jerry talked to them from the microphone and I never understood a word he said, so that became even funnier. Of course, only about 75% of the house stuck around to see how in the hell we were going to manage the rest of the show.

For the most part, Jerry Gropp was a total professional. We had a lot in common and he taught me much about showmanship and how a visual impression can be a huge part of any performance.

By this time, when a high level of talent showed up on my front step, I had learned to recognize it and take notice. During the early 70's, I had the pure pleasure of working for some time with Jimmy Grey, Dave Gibson and Vern Andrews. These 3 talented musicians/performers challenged me and brought about one of the biggest learning curves of all time. It also groomed me for the demands of road work.

In the 80's, I started a band project called, Stumpwater-Jak with Jerry Gropp on lead vocals, it turned out to be a very successful band. Gropp toured some 20 years with Waylon Jennings before going to Canada and producing several hit records of his own. The first night ever together was with Paul Stout on guitar as well. He had the house band at Pinnacle Peak in Scottsdale and could not give up the helm for a startup project. Bobby Sidelman on drums had some health issues at the time so I called in Mike Hounshell to round out the trio.

The Hammrick family of North Phoenix put up front money for Stumpwater-Jak to record an album. We recorded at Pantheon Studio's in Scottsdale. The results were nothing short of surreal. When the album was released, we had what seemed like an overnight hit with the song "Too Many Outlaws".

KNIX, the local Buck Owens country radio station, picked up the song and it went "A" rotation for over 12 weeks. Not only did Buck's sons, Buddy Allen and

Mike Owens push the recording but the afternoon drive time jock, Jim West, stayed behind the song as well. Jim and I have remained good friends for well over 30 years.

Jim could be called an historian of early Rock-a-Billy and Arizona country music. Jim West is sharing the knowledge of Arizona's music legends. His book will give readers a special glimpse back at the great early desert country music leaders who put Arizona on the music industry map. Hopefully he will include much of the explosive era of Outlaw Country during the 70's & 80's.

On a rare night off after Jerry went back to Waylon's band, I went to Sedona and caught a show featuring Johnny Western. His delivery was very professional and everything about it was impressive. I was going to leave without saying hello. That's when that gut-feeling I'd learned to listen to kicked in. I went over and introduced myself to Johnny. He knew of the band's recent success so I only left him a short verbal resume and phone number. It turned out to be a highly interesting conversation with me learning among other things, that Waylon Jennings had introduced him to his wife, Jo.

Johnny Western had worked with Johnny Cash for many years. He also had a stellar history in LA working in the television industry. He appeared in movies and many TV western series such as Bonanza and Have Gun, Will Travel. He signed with Columbia Records and wrote sound tracks for TV westerns, the most famous being the theme for Have Gun, Will Travel which has been named the #1 TV Western Theme Song of all Time.

Within a few short months after I had introduced myself at the Sedona concert, Johnny called and hired me as his Band Leader and bass player in a new group he was forming. We called ourselves The Arizona Rangers. What I learned from watching Johnny's talents over the years while on the road gave me a foundation that has made my life better in so many ways. It has been my good fortune to be able to call Johnny Western a lifelong friend. I also had the honor of standing next to him on a stage in Willcox, Az when it was announced he was to be inducted into the Arizona Music and Entertainment Hall of Fame along with Rex Allen Jr. his good friend. I got to help produce the Johnny Western induction ceremony at the Western Museum in Scottsdale Arizona.

A real blessing in disguise was running into a great player by the name of Hal Monti. He has a super attitude about life and the music business. A really good guitar player who always wanted the product to be as good as it could be. Hal called one afternoon and asked me to come down to his gig that evening and meet a young man with great potential as a front man, singer, and entertainer.

When I arrived at the club, it dawned on me this was also an audition. I was so taken back by the energy level and with a dedicated direction shown by this young man, Ron Keel, that when I was offered a job with the band, my answer was an immediate yes.

We began a quick climb and started receiving major recognition at warp speed. Ron was not new being in the spotlight. He and his band, KEEL, had world-wide exposure during the big hair metal rock era in LA. Ron could sing, play guitar, drums, and write music in any format as well as, if not better than anyone I'd ever met. He possessed a passion that became more contagious as the weeks rolled on. I learned more in one year about the music business, integrity and staying focused on goals than I had ever seen before.

The first project with Ron was called the Ronnie Lee Keel band, then we later worked another year together in the Las Vegas market with a show he developed called Country Superstars Tribute. When Ron put on the goatee, mustache and created Ronnie Dunn's persona on stage, the resemblance, visually and vocally, was uncanny. The Brooks and Dunn hit parade had been in full swing for well over 15 years so marketing this type of show was nothing short of genius. With a little make up and some learned mannerisms, Ron produced an outstanding tribute to one of the best tenors Ronnie Dunn ever in Country Music.

Working with Ron in Las Vegas took me to an even greater level of performance abilities. Many great Las Vegas musicians also took the time to help me during that time. Joe Sparker, a stellar keyboard player, Tommy Wayne, an incredible steel guitar man, Craig Small on drums, Kevin Curry, another fantastically talented producer and guitar player. Professional performances by Brian Pop, Cory Sacks, Kathy Wollf, Dave Hoover, Roy Hammerik, and many others made a lasting impression.

It had already been a long trip back from where I had been in combat during the late 60's. By 1970 the Vietnam War was still fresh in my mind and I was in trouble. I found out about marijuana by chance from another combat veteran. We were talking about the madness of re-adjustment upon returning from war. I mentioned my reckless behavior behind the wheel and starting fights at the drop of a hat. It was a crazy time period for me. I think my ole neighborhood buddy knew I was in deep trouble.

We walked into his back room one day in late 1969 and he grabbed a handful of Cambodian Red marijuana out of a stuffed sea bag. When he opened it, I saw there was a blue lined heavy mill plastic bag inside the duffle bag. I said, "shit-man that's a body bag from Vietnam". He smiled and told me he received about one of these every month. My childhood friend jammed some strange smelling buds into a baggie and told me to trust him. What he was giving me would settle me down so I could function in society.

It basically saved my life; I was spinning out of control barely skirting the police from calls and complaints from people saying I was disturbing the peace. Some 30 years later, I tried to track the man down and thank him for helping me get through that time of my life but I could never locate him. Here now, in real time, the government and many doctors, psychologists and others in the medical field, have come to realize marijuana could help PTSD and other ailments our society deals with.

There was a time in the early 80's when all the shows I did at Coliseums, arenas, Concert Halls and stadiums seemed to blur together in one continuous dream. Doing shows with the top entertainers of the era on a weekly basis and doing one continuous party played a wrecking game with my personal life also. We were being given cocaine like it was candy. On many occasions, when we checked-in at a venue, a full baggie each of pot and cocaine were our welcome gifts. It didn't take long until I was using on a regular basis. More than occasionally, I wound up snorting more than I had earned that night.

This behavior went on for about 3 years until one day I had what I now call the morning of reckoning if you will. Staying up until the wee hours of the morning one time the house mortgage paperwork had gotten spread. I had stayed up after the gig one night and had it all figured out. I would take out a second mortgage on my house. I only needed about 20K to accomplish my plan. I would buy a couple of kilos, cut it, and then resell it to buy back the loan. Oh, and keeping the rest of the cocaine for my free personal use.

The next morning I stared at the pile of paper on the kitchen table for some time as the smell of fresh coffee filled the noon air. Something suddenly shifted in my head and I knew my life had spiraled out of control and I was in serious trouble. I got dressed, gathered up my related drug paraphernalia and put it in a paper bag. That bag included glass chopping mirrors, strainers, small bottles, little spoons, pipes and anything that supported a drug habit. I drove over to the dealer's house and asked him if he would take everything in the sack to call it even on my drug bill. It was a fair trade and he said sure. I never again took another hit of cocaine or any drug other than pot since that day in 1983.

Friends I knew at the time continued on with their addictions for many, many years. It was just my good fortune that the strong will and conviction of that terrible feeling I had experienced that morning stayed in my memory and reared up every time another opportunity to slip came my way.

Some 10 years later, I was able to summon the same determination to quit cigarettes, as well. In my opinion, the later was the most difficult to quit. But, again after having made up my mind, I never again touched another cigarette.

Am I fortunate to have the ability to quit addictive vices at will? I'm not sure. But I do know that bad habits can be controlled with a positive mind set and determination.

In Vietnam most of the locals were addicted to Betelnut; a leafy form of plant that produces some sort of a high. I was told it was like drinking 5 quick cups of strong coffee all at once. I never tried it because the plant causes a dark stain and users get black stained teeth from continued use.

When I returned to the states and was released back into civilian life, the big craze was small white pills called "Truckers White Cross's". I could work 2 or 3 jobs a day with the kind of energy they mustered. Some guys were eating 6 to 8 pills at a time. For me, splitting one in half and running like a track star all day proved it did not take much for me to be affected. When I got down to about 135 pounds at 5'8" tall, I decided it might be best to go ahead and have an appetite. Well, for America's youthful recreational drug users, they moved on to more exotic forms.

There was a time when I could throw back some tequila and beer at a good clip. But after almost passing out while driving east through the Papago mountain range in Phoenix early one morning, I came to grips with drinking alcohol. When I woke up about four hours later just as the sun was rising behind me, I remembered falling to the right onto the bench seat of my car, putting one foot on the break and pushing the gear up to park with my right hand while laying on my side just in time. It only took me thinking, Wow that really happened? Never did that again either.

I was about 25 years old at the time that happened and went totally sober from that point on for about 5 years. If having fun meant getting passed out drunk I wanted no part of it. Somewhere in my travels I think when I was around 30, I finally realized it would be okay for me to have a social beer or two on occasion.

Survival can be luck and it surely was for me on many occasions. It is up to the individual to recognize these free passes' and make correct decisions going forward.

Most of my close calls were not necessarily recognized as suicidal tendencies. But maybe, in a way they were. After surviving combat and close calls under extremely dangerous conditions, a combat veteran tends to live life to its fullest every day.

There is a period after deployment when a level headed friend, concerned relative or Vet Center needs to monitor the veteran's adjustment back into civilian life. It is also up to the individual to put aside pride and allow some guidance from available sources. We are all ultimately responsible for our actions. The life we save could be our own.

Many returning vets appear to be doing fine. But we, as a society, must pay attention. It's important to find a way to exorcise any lurking demons combat veterans may have so the horror of deeds experienced in the name of freedom will not have delayed affects.

When the world started shutting down around me after my enlistment was over, I had music to keep me company. When people in my age group as well as younger civilians strongly indicate they do not want to hear about war, a combat veteran can feel unappreciated and unworthy. After all, it was such a daunting experience for them. Why wouldn't everyone want to hear about the tragic ordeal in that foreign land? It took decades for me to realize and accept that's just the way it is.

After wife number 2 left me, there was a period of time when every moment of solitude was spent playing guitar at home alone. I would listen to cassette tapes one after the other until I had memorized every song and could play it as well as the recording.

I sincerely believe that all veterans need that type of passionate interest to occupy their minds and help in their survival tactics.

A new organization named Guitars for Veterans is about the best program I've heard of in a long time. There will be other good ideas and programs surfacing now all the time. A family member or a veteran can champion these causes and help save lives.

Here are a few of the latest links to help veterans and PTSD patients in general. Some may fall off the grid but others will join the trend of helping.

Links to help PTSD and related Issue's

Emergency Help Hotline   1-(800) 273-8255

National Veteran help hot line link for all services.
http://www.veteranscrisisline.net/

Helping Vets Connect: http://www.veteranshelpinghands.com/

Guitars for Veterans http://www.guitars4vets.org/

Veterans PTSD help web page https://www.veteransptsd.org/

www.va.gov/health/NewsFeatures/2013/May/PTSD-Help-With-You-When-You-Need-It-Most.asp

Testimonial; www.wnyc.org story/93503-music-helps-vets-control-symptoms-ptsd/

Music Therapy for Vets; http://www.musictherapyforvets.com/

How to Help a Friend; http://www.heal-post-traumatic-stress.com/help-PTSD-sufferer.html

PTSD Help Network; http://ptsdhelp.net/index.html

All Trauma Help; http://helpguide.org/home-pages/ptsd-trauma.htm

Help with PTSD; http://www.healthjourneys.com/ptsd.asp

PTSD Support; http://ptsdsupport.net/

Therapy; http://www.goodtherapy.org/therapy-for-ptsd.html#

www.medicalmarijuana.com/medical-marijuana-treatments/
Post-Traumatic-Stress-Disorder-PTSD

A Manuel on PTSD; http://www2.nami.org/Content/ContentGroups/Programs/
Family_to_Family/PTSD_Module_Pevised_Feb_2011.pdf

Combat Veteran Job Transition Help"
http://www.military.com/veteran-jobs/career-advice/resume-writing/resume-
tips-for-making-the-transition-to-private-industry.html

In time these links may not be available. Some research can be exercised for updating support groups offered over the internet. Consult the VA for new and improved services recommended.

A SWORD OF HONOR

In 2006 my neighbor across the street, an E-5 in the Arizona National Guard, just returned from his second tour in Iraq as a military policeman. They were the ones doing the house-to-house routing out insurgents. He is a standup solider for sure. Between his tours we swapped stories in my front yard about my Vietnam tour in 1966. How it was not unlike his actions through these small communities in the current war zone. I explained about the (6th-sense) thing, stay alert at all times, and watch your men very carefully. We emailed each other often during his tour as I swapped pep phrases and words of encouragement. During his last couple of weeks in the war zone during his second tour he took on a mentoring position with his squad and others just arriving. Urging them to stay alert and go with your instincts. One "new to country" PFC asked him, what have you done to survive your past two tours? Keith tells me he put his head down and thought for a short time. He told me he said that listening to the advice and silent guidance of strength from a Marine Vietnam Veteran back home helped. That he learned to pay attention to his (6th-sense), and did not stray from his objectives. Keith would gather his men around the computer and let them read my emails. They started visiting our bands website, and saw that we were doing music shows at the Veterans Hospitals in our home state. I am happy to say that all of his men rotated back to the Phoenix area safe during that tour and without bodily injuries.

Keith got home Friday the 23rd of June 2006. His family and fiancé came to one of our shows on a Saturday night. They listened to a set of spirited music, and appreciating the audience's response to his return from the war zone. On our first break I sprinted over to their table for handshakes. I held up fairly well until out from under the table came a long box. Keith said my squad and I want you to have this. Opening the box, I retrieved a beautiful United States NCO Marine Sword.

Keith explained we were sweeping an area on the outskirts of Baghdad, when this family could not truthfully explain what they were doing with it. Keith's men confiscated the sword and took it back to their tents. They realized that it would be a daunting task to identify its true origin, so later that night they all agreed that it would go back to Prescott Valley, Arizona. To be displayed in the house of a Vietnam Marine that gave them so much survival wisdom. At that point I became humbled to no end, and will always remember the wonderful gesture these warriors of a new generation made for this Vietnam Veteran.

The next day we took turns swapping war stories on my front porch over sweet tea and peanuts. We established that not a word of recalling these close encounters were to get out to dad across the street. If they did, his father would get upset and the effects could be extremely discomforting for his parents.

One story in particular churned up as we talked thru the afternoon. I was very interested to understand the current war from his perspective. But I could not believe while I compared how different the times were. Transportation to the war zone was now by way of airplane. Soldiers were assigned tasks at warp speed by comparison to my era.

In 1966 we went over to Vietnam by ship. The USS Paul Revere was slow and boring to put it mildly. I've mentioned some of the good times so now I will recall an incident that has repeatedly played out in my mind since the day it happened

The beachhead landing to disembark a ship full of Marines is surely a task even the participants only know very little about. One might understand a particular part of the event but complex must be a seemingly mild adjective of description

We had some boot camp training of climbing up the nets, and then down the other side so a little muscle memory was somewhat in place. Over the nets loaded down with a full backpack of belongings, an M-14 rifle, and some heavy parts of an M-60 machine gun. Going over the side of this ship only seemed normal business because the Marines in front of you were headed over themselves. There was nothing familiar about the strength it took to fight the force of gravity while hanging on to that net with all that weight

The seas were extremely choppy that day so the ship was rising and falling from the waters in rhythmic fashion with some predictability. By the time I got close to the landing craft below, the swells difference in height could be as much as 8 feet. The men above you had no concept of paying attention to a method of timing your drop to minimize the fall. Why, because the men above them, were repelling faster than you could give them room.

Men were stepping on my hands, shoulders, and arms. I was screaming for everyone to pay attention below. One has to time the "let go" for safety. Much too noisy was the operation to comprehend such a logical awareness. The added weight became too much to bear. When I landed on my back looking up at the net I had just came from, it seemed like a dream. A few Marines helped me to my feet while guided me to one side as to accept the remainder that were assigned to this red china sea water taxi to the beach

While gathered on the beach we overheard that 8 Marines were lost in the rough seas along with some vehicles and supplies. It took another day for the bruises to show up from the fall. I can remember thinking it would be great if we never had to do that again. That wish came true as I finished my career of riding on boats that maneuvered over the ocean. I have not since, and will never get on a boat that calls any ocean it's home. The helplessness one feels while starring over the edge of a railing in the middle of an ocean has been permanently imprinted in my mind. The thought of having to exit a ship again in a similar fashion has paralyzed any ambition of riding on a vacation cruse or a fishing excursion

This sixth sense thing that had been cultivating from as far back as I can remember came to light in the Oklahoma hills one day. While navigating the streets of Phoenix as a youth it (the sixth sense) was to avoid a cranky neighbors dog. Possibility it was that dangerous situation at an intersection of fast moving cars that I avoided. The many times I walked home as a youth after dark, sometimes just taking another route. I somehow just learned to recognize the sixth sense thing when it appeared. That was all I was trying to relay to my Army veteran across the street. I seemed to bring it to his attention at every chance we had. It was either on the Internet while he was in the combat zone, or when wc talked during his frequenl visils back home during his three tours

We lived way back in the hills close to the Arkansas border in a community called Bunch, Oklahoma. It was a beautiful spring day as the setting sun cast long shadows through the hilly woods. The many birds, insects, subtle sounds of the forest, and life itself suddenly vanished. The moment caught me off guard as I came to an abrupt halt. It was a surprisingly intense awareness of the changing moment that brought a high sense of concern. I froze except for my eyes, and the slightest moves back and forth with my head. Scanning every inch of the forest in a pattern of 10 yards in front of me at each 180 degree passing. It went on and on for a long time. Not being able to even press my weight forward in preparation for a step was possible. Out at the 30 yard area in front of me perfectly straight ahead came the reason. I was headed straight for a freshly born litter of wolf pups.

There was a slight breeze blowing at my back. My scent and the rustle of foot steps must have startled the pack to some degree. It appeared they did not have enough time to react as they were in a semi circle of protection around the litter. After realizing that walking forward would have been a disaster I was perfectly still

It was two or three minutes later when I came to understand just backing out of there was the correct action. Calmness came over me just before I started moving backwards. When danger left my presence it felt as if somehow I had just communicated with the Universe. It was a good feeling of satisfaction, that whole thing with awareness for correction. This incident was remembered and must have helped me deal with situations in combat and life for many years to come

I became visibly concerned that afternoon while talking to my neighbor's son when he told me he was considering going back for another tour. He had a very unique job description that takes confidence and trust to be assigned. Therefor he felt it necessary to return. It does become a personal thing with combat veterans

The commitment to the war effort from men of his caliber during this era is where the word bravery resides. The United States Army got a good man with this enlistment. He has gone on to make a career out of the military. A prime example of why this country is worth defending is documented in family histories similar to my neighbors. The luxuries of freedom we all get to benefit are earned from many brave families throughout history just like this one

I will enjoy this sword from the Wyman family that spent a tour in Iraq. It will be passed on to my family as a reminder that defending our countries rights came with sacrifice. The ideal of America was well earned, and all honorable citizens should be thankful for the effort of previous generations.

When Keith returned from his 3rd tour he relayed a story that unfolded during an operation. A keen reminder of why the Sixth Sense and intuition needs a front row seat during times of responsibility or routine

Upon leaving a group of Iraqi fighters to defend the evening's camp he perched his observation post where he could keep an eye on them plus the forward action. During an early morning hour he observed with night vision lens a movement by them towards the opposite direction his orders had stated. He confronted that action in private by reporting to his commanders their secret agenda.

The observance uncovered deeper implications of the Iraqi resistance towards their so called American alliance. It was my understanding the incident was dealt with in a swift penetrating authority. The damage levels of betrayal among the locals were now exposed. His sixth sense and full time commitment to the assignments actions were followed. If not, it most likely could have resulted in many future horrific situations

The locals want peace and liberty, but are unwilling to betray their countrymen's radical brand of justice. Just like in the Vietnam War you never knew if the daytime players put on a different mask after dark. The local farmers and residents living close to our camp sites would drop in during the day. For me it was easy to see some of them were casing the layout

The happy ending is that Keith has survived his 4 tours in tack and will now look forward to a military retirement and return to American Civilian Liberties. The level of intensity he learned to achieve will follow him into his next phase of life. This is where the problems start to manifest. It has become the norm to distrust all.

But now with my neighbor's son talks have taken on another agenda. It is not over, not by a long shot. It all seems fine for now, but the horror of war and the assignment of survival is an ongoing never ending maintenance issue.

We all will need the professional VA guidance that has now started to filter into the hospitals and Vet Centers across America. I would like to suggest that all war zone veterans take advantage of the new commitment and direction being offered. There are family programs that include the spouse and or parents and support groups. The big mistake would be to think that you are immune to the affects. Oh, I've got this from here could be a selfish action to your loved ones that are suppressing opinions.

My deepest depression about war deployment and the things endured over there came some 40 years after the fact. They were always present, but just not recognized as the reason I was this way. Being a bit of a paranoid loaner has an ear mark of a century out on his post. It just feels like your duty station.

It's only normal over there in the combat zone. It becomes destructive over time back home because the sheer numbers around you have not been exposed to that level of survival mode. You are just different, and it will always be that way. As soon as I admitted that it was OK to seek help by taking the criticism, a better person emerged.

WHAT ARE WE DOING HERE?

As I gazed out over the starboard side of the USS Paul Revere in full gear my thoughts were all about us saving this country from the communist aggressors. The Red China Sea was fighting us back with much more resistance than the enemy that day. There were huge angry white caps crashing into the hull of the troop carrier causing the ship to sway back and forth. Not that noticeable on deck, but when you looked over the edge at the smaller landing crafts it was obviously going to be a challenge.

Boot camp training from stationary obstacle courses with perfect nets and ropes is not what was before me. I stood on the side waiting my turn to crawl over with my gear. There was major difference of movement at the landing craft from one second to the next.

I tried to comprehend the big picture as I grasped to take in the overwhelming size of this task. It looked like a movie I had seen, not one that I was in. Youth has no fear.

It seemed like only a couple of weeks earlier we were preparing for final exams as senior's in High school. I felt patriotic pride each night during that time while watching old war movies from the 40's on TV. My enlistment and soon departure for the Marine Corps would make a big difference. Boot Camp was only a month away so the anticipation of going to Vietnam was real. Nightly news reports of the American occupation build up were sandwiched between Beatle Mania and Ricky Nelson episodes.

It was a major task getting this division of Marines on shore. We convoyed in land to our objective on the outskirts of Hue. I could not help but judge how these people were living. We went through little villages of grass huts, dirt floors, dirty kids playing in the paths of scooters and old French economy cars.

White smoke from the fireplaces of the village hooch's drifted skyward. Women cooking mid-day meals could be seen in every hamlet. Along the way groups of kids waving all the while begging for throw me downs of C rations and candy. Smiling faces in the front rows were catching the eye of most Marines as we rolled along.

That's not all that was noticed by me as I looked beyond the surface. In the back rows I saw the few elders, and young women with body language that spelled NO.....we don't like you.....you are the invaders. They seemed poised to turn and run with the slightest possibility that we might stop in their hamlet and start milling around.

We would soon find out that most of them stashed rice, ammunition, and supplies just on the outskirts of their ancient communities. They had to as aggression from both sides to support the cause meant survival. While in route that day it all hit me at once. What are we doing here trying to save these people? They don't want to be saved, they look perfectly happy with their fake smiles and waves as we motored by.

My first taste of a third world country other than on TV was an eye opener. The village people had black teeth from the beetle nut leaves staining over the years. They were bare footed and they had plain styled black or white cloth just hanging from their frail body frames. Skinny little people that looked under nourished. They had no corner stores like theatres, gas stations, schoolyards, traffic lights, hotels, and golf courses. There is nothing we can do for these people.

Below is a speech by John F. Kennedy he delivered 10 years prior to America's serious desire to occupy and suppress the North Vietnams takeover of the South.

> "I am frankly of the belief that no amount of American military assistance in Indochina can conquer an enemy which is everywhere and at the same time nowhere, 'an enemy of the people' which has the sympathy and covert support of the people...In November of 1951, I reported upon my return from the Far East as follows: 'In Indochina we have allied ourselves to the desperate effort of a French regime to hang on to the remnants of empire. There is no broad, general support of the native Vietnam Government among the people of that area... [To try to win military victory] apart from and in defiance of innately nationalistic aims spells foredoomed failure.'"
> **– Senator John F. Kennedy**, 1954

> It would take some research and time for me to someday realize the propaganda and direction of Red China and Russia. They were making it apparent their purpose. To dominate all of Southeast Asia by having a steady stream

of supplies to the South through the North of Vietnam is all they need to create alliance with the people.

Just because America felt it noble and courageous that the French had taken a bold stand in the region for democracy should not have been a reason to align with such a campaign.

John Kennedy was never in favor on helping in Vietnam. Most opinions in his camp were totally against it. Companies that stand to gain from the product it would take to support a war in that country were many. Their lobbyists would soon launch an aggressive program with our United States individual politicians.

Although in the same year that Kennedy delivered his foredoomed failure essay Vice-President Richard Nixon seemed to have a slightly different mindset. In April of that year he was quoted as believing more men are needed to support the French in Vietnam. He said the Vietnamese lack the ability to conduct a war by itself. So America's current administration must face up to the communist escalation and dispatch troops. Some believe this language served as a green light for investors to shake it up and gear it up for the next war to begin.

Soon after the convoy to base camp at Phu Bi just outside of Hue, Vietnam I participated in an assignment to support a forward observation point. We were on a two or three day event aboard a 6X truck when we arrived on the out skirts of a small village. It would have been close to Hue as I sat on the far back seat by the tailgate.

With my M-14 rifle between my knees I noticed a small motorbike coming up behind us. The Vietnamese male driver had a young oriental girl hanging on to his waist. It was obvious he was trying to show off his riding skills by weaving back and forth trying to pass this huge 10-wheel transport truck.

The scooter driver became impatient following us so he began passing on the right side. As they passed very close I couldn't help but notice the innocent youthful faces. It was at that exact time I felt the trucks acceleration suddenly drop. Then sure enough, we were turning right. I crinkled my nose and frowned at the other Marines who were all looking at me as if I could have done something.

The bike and two riders entered under our troop transport truck behind the front tire area as we started a right hand turn. We could hear their bodies bouncing and crunching off the undercarriage below our feet. They both exited in a mangled mess before my eyes at the tailgate. We came to an immediate stop as I peered down at the mayhem. Their lifeless expressions became frozen in time for the next hour, days, and years to come.

Village folks gathered around waiting with anguish as two of their young folks perished before their eyes. There were no sirens, or first responders. Our corpsman went to both young people kneeling while shaking his head. There was nothing we could do except compromise our assignment by staying. I've seen this incident play out many times and have never forgotten the helplessness of the primitive life some countries really have.

This was one of the first realizations that war causes much causality that are not attributed directly to the battlefield. Tropical disease overcame many or our military in Vietnam. There was an extremely horrific fire aboard the USS Forestall on the open sea while in support of this war. The duty a combat solider fulfills in the name of the operation never goes away. These wounds are real, and in many cases will surface years later in guilt ridden minds.

The redirection of focus among our youth when returned to their homeland in many cases was not a healthy path. PTSD is a growing fungus like cancer in your body. It is hard to detect in its infancy, but very determined to intensify as time goes by. Combat veterans came home to a country that did not want to hear about it. They melded back into society with these memories just under the sanity zone. They appeared just fine to most, but close family members saw the drastic changes in their war serving men and women.

The tragedy occurred when the need for help never came. There were no programs in place to support Veterans. Even in the bigger cities counselors were a token gesture to the lucky few. There was very little help available for the returning front line enlisted man struggling to find a job. Employment and career opportunities in many cases were not offered from the scared media opinionated public sector. Stories of gone crazy veterans made headlines as success stories in spite of; took decades to finally surface.

The first time I heard the words Welcome Home came some 40 years after returning from combat. When the words were spoken a release of emotion and pent up sorrow coupled with a feeling of forgiveness seemed to surface. It feels nice to finally get the recognition at the same time hoping that our next generation of combat veterans will not endure the same shameful loneliness.

While I struggled inside to make sense of it all trying to re enter in to civilian life the same question would arise. What are we doing here? Many war Veterans must have naturally received the healing necessary by diving head first into the good fortunes that came their way. Many did not! I always felt like my innocence remained in that country. The natural development from childhood to adulthood without a combat experience had to have at least more than a blink or two in between.

The extreme good fortune of having music in my life became a savior of circumstances. There could not have been a gig; big or small go by without me being marveled at how lucky I was to be participating in the music industry. Musicians are in a small world when you maneuver around the profession trying to make a living at it. It paid the bills for many years, and helped to raise children during that time.

I've also had the good fortune of hanging out with some of the most interesting people at different times. In one way or another they all had a part in saving me from either financial blunder or psychological disaster.

Music was a wonderful profession through the 60's, 70's & 80's. Live entertainment was flourishing so the demand was high and the participants were many. If allowed club owners, and musicians in the Phoenix area to excel and enjoy tremendous success.

The Instant gratification of an appreciative audience after a song or show is a healing act in itself. This was something not experienced in combat. In war we were all expected to do our job, our part, our duty then move on to the next assignment. In music I found comfort in not only possessing the mental ability to play music, but the recognition that came with it.

Deprived of acceptance upon returning from combat in the Vietnam war was factoring in another level of pain to overcome. Suppressing the experience within our lives became a way of life. Personally feeling the need to prove self-worth on a continued agenda became a driving force. For many with no direction or release it surly must have created overwhelming out of control anger.

Around the end of, and directly after the Vietnam War a very unfortunate pattern surfaced with some Veterans who did not see combat up close. It also included many men who did not serve at all, but learned enough dialogue to fool the many who would listen.

A book was introduced many years later called Stolen Valor. The read was loaned to me by a VA counselor in early 2000. It shed much light on why the true Vietnam Vets were the forgotten warriors. I became very angry after reading the book and expressed that with deep conviction. It also seems many non-veterans used a pretend enlistment to explain their in ability to function in a normal society. They did not want to work, nor did they want to earn worldly possessions. By claiming they were war veterans they stole the respect of the many that did deserve it.

No level of our society was off limits. Politicians claimed outrageous tours of duty to get elected on a false "we owe it to him" platform. CEO's of many major companies had fake military records hidden in their HR files.

Once the gig was up they started falling like dominos. Many just came out and told the truth before being discovered. Many took shelter in relocation with a fresh start using the experience they earned by moving elsewhere with a clean slate. Disgust and anger mixed with just sadness for the real war survivors came over me for many months after reading that book. The guilt experienced by the betrayers had to have filtered into their families.

The thought of what am I doing here is a huge priority after reaching what some consider a mortality phase of their lives. Of course it's never too late to start a project that would make a huge difference to society or your family's legacy for that matter. For me it became very clear that looking back on my accomplishments to date, could hold some inspiration or answers to the question.

Rather than being remembered for just the service to my country, the ability to survive with a measure of success under the circumstances is as much a noble achievement.

Worrying about one's mortality can be a dangerous undertaking. It is not something I recommend doing on your own. Unless you have a good grip on the exercise it could start a chain reaction that leads to a very dark place. One thing for certain is how one can question your mortality when it's never really been put to the real test.

There have been some extraordinary accomplishments through life after combat for many Americans in our country's history. Just getting through high school was pure determination and luck for me. Having an experience in the Marine Corps and capitalizing on all of its opportunities like I did was a blessing. This exceptionally rewarding musical career I've had is what dreams are made of. The financial gain and ability of leadership in the construction world has been a pleasant surprise.

Survival with a measure of success is all anyone can hope for. We have all made some bad choices then rebounded. It is the continuation of challenge that makes us strong and wise enough to see opportunity coming then take advantage. A combat tour is a major bump in the road for sure, but if you do not let it overwhelm or define you, it could work in your favor.

I believe asking the question why am I here can serve to help us focus on priorities. It also may help to find humor and insight into direction, then motivation. If you have accomplished a task to your best ability and served its purpose consider moving on to the next challenge. After all, sometimes it's the chase that can be the reward vs. the bounty.

We all must spend our time on earth doing what makes us feel good. It's not a dress rehearsal you see. Its one time around the block so making the best of things is the only logical answer.

You have a story about war that could benefit many or just one person. We are all connected, but at the same time unique. Your war & memories need to be documented. They could be about how you survived a completely dysfunctional family life. It could have been coping with a father of combat PTSD.

Parents that abused drugs or over indulged in drink or gambling could have similar effects of survival. The fact you have survived with a measure of success is inspiring in itself.

Your story could inspire someone to stop the destructive pattern of abusing themselves. That though alone gave me tremendous inspiration to produce this memoir. The statistics are showing some 22 veterans per day are committing suicide due to PTSD symptoms. How many non-combat veterans are doing the same because of pent up depression caused by destructive lifestyle parents that received no help?

If we can all find some humor, achievement, and reasons for stepping up to the plate every day with a positive attitude it could make all the difference. Most of my fondest memories are of helping someone else have a great day. I've often thought that just remembering someone's name could make all the difference.

I've always believed that it's really all about, "Survival with a measure of Success"